C000221658

Designing for Special Needs

an architect's guide to briefing and designing options for living for people with learning disabilities

Maurice Harker and Nigel King
for The Shirley Foundation

RIBA Enterprises

© The Shirley Foundation, 2002

Published by RIBA Enterprises Ltd, 1-3 Dufferin Street,
London EC1Y 8NA

ISBN 1 85946 121 2

Product Code: 27536

The rights of the Authors to be identified as the Authors of this work have been asserted in accordance with the Copyright, Designs and Patents Act 1988.

All rights reserved. No part of this publication may be reproduced, stored in a retrieval system, or transmitted, in any form or by any means, electronic, mechanical, photocopying, recording or otherwise, without the prior permission of the copyright owner.

British Library Cataloguing in Publication Data.
A catalogue record of this book is available from the British Library.

Publisher: Mark Lane
Commissioning Editor: Matthew Thompson
Project Editor: Katy Banyard
Editor: Elizabeth Davison
Design: Ilze Van der Poll

Typeset, printed and bound by Hobbs the Printers, Hampshire

While every effort has been made to check the accuracy of the information given in this book, readers should always make their own checks. Neither the Authors nor the Publisher accepts any responsibility for mis-statements made in it or misunderstandings arising from it.

Contents

Foreword

This book is for amateurs like me who are concerned, and often struggle, to provide quality living for people with learning disabilities, and for architects, designers and other professionals dealing with the same issues.

The authors, Maurice Harker and Nigel King, have distilled their personal and professional experiences into an inspirational yet practical sourcebook of information. Would that it had been available when I first set up a small group home for adults who, like my son, had profound learning disabilities. It is not so long ago that such people were expected to live in significantly sub-standard accommodation.

But in this new century, Care in the Community rightly has aspirations for everyone to live in dignity and comfort. This needs plumbers to plumb efficiently, builders to build with attentive caution, architects to plan around all the additional needs - the list is long but the plumbers come first, because modern civilisation is founded on plumbing that works and my experience is that many unnecessary costs are associated with plumbing that doesn't.

Cost is always important, but it is values and value for money that have been at the heart of this RIBA project since its inception in 1999. And I am delighted that, in future, professional practices will be able to provide this publication for handy reference by every architect and every planner.

The grant-giving Shirley Foundation selects and monitors its charitable projects to be pioneering by nature and strategic in impact. It has therefore been a pleasure and a privilege to sponsor this timely publication. My co-trustees join me in hoping that it will help to provide a better lifestyle for people with special needs, whatever their needs and wherever they choose to live.

Dame Stephanie Shirley
The Shirley Foundation

Acknowledgements

We are very grateful for the information provided by the following organisations:

Advance Housing and Support, Witney; Andrews Partnership, Crowthorne; Broadway Malyan Architects, Theale; Derek Rogers Associates, Tring; Edwin Trotter Associates; Evans Jones Partners, Cheltenham; Hightown Praetorian Housing Association, Hemel Hempstead; Leeds Federated Housing Association; New Dimension Group, Theale; Pavilion Publishing, Brighton; Pentahact, Barnet; Simon Humphreys, Simon Humphreys Architects, London; Southern Focus Trust, Portsmouth; Technology in Healthcare, Anglesey; The Joseph Rowntree Foundation; The Priors Court Foundation, Newbury; Tim Ralphs Design Group, Birmingham; United Response, London; West and Machell Architects, Leeds; Autism West Midlands and Coddington School.

And to the following individuals for their advice and contributions to the study:

Stuart Allcock; Dr David Bonnett; Tony Dixon; Dr Kevin Doughty; Nigel Faiers; Melvin Gardiner; Graham Jackson; Colin Keegan; Martin Nicholas; Mike Ormian; Nick Price and Su Sayer.

MH
NK

List of figures

1. Introduction

1.1 The need for information on design

This guide is primarily concerned with where and how people live, with residential and housing options of several kinds. The guide also looks at residential accommodation as part of a school and gives an idea of designing for an establishment, a school or college. Though the featured case studies are all in England, much of the guidance will be of use for the UK in general.

People with learning disabilities are people first and there are many whose main requirement is an ordinary home. Others want an ordinary home too but for reasons of their disability, health, physical, support or management requirements, the design of their home deserves particular care. As with designing for people with physical disabilities, the first rule is to recognise and pay attention to the diversity of individual needs.

There is very little recent guidance of any kind on designing for people with learning disabilities. Earlier design guidance on learning disability has tended to be based on residential care models, often led by standards developed for older people. Another view is that using existing housing stock is the best option and special design unnecessary. Neither of these approaches is adequate.

Professional consultants, service funders and commissioners, developers and managers, and local carers groups find little in published guidance to inform their planning process and design solutions. There are important matters of procedure, good practice, minimum standards, statutory requirements, special needs and design solutions, which it would be useful to bring together. Both client and consultant will benefit and avoid learning everything the hard way. This guide brings together the experience and special expertise of practitioners to make the most of present knowledge in this field.

1.2 Who this guide is written for

The choice of publisher suggests the importance of reaching architectural consultants and surveyors, but the guide should also be relevant for housing and support providers, housing associations, health authorities and trusts, local authority commissioners in housing and social services, national and local charities, voluntary and carer (including parent) organisations, Mencap and Autistic Society groups. Architects, project developers and their consultants often feel they are beginning work without proper guidance or sources on which to draw. This can lead to expensive or faulty results.

1.3 Scope of this guide

This guide deals with accommodation, with housing options for people with special needs. Guidance for the National Health Service and the Community Care Act 1990[1] stated that the aim is 'to enable people to live as normal a life as possible in their own home or in a homely environment in the community'.

The Government has recently produced a White Paper[2] on learning disability, *Valuing People*, the first for 30 years. The government objective is 'To enable people with learning disabilities and their families to have greater choice and control over where and how they live'. The Government wants the development of a range of housing options. Housing and social services are asked to work together to expand housing, care and support options.

Health and social services already spend about £2.5 billion on residential support for people with learning disabilities but there has been no published guidance on design since 1983. More people are expected to be able to live in ordinary homes in the community rather than hospitals, but this will only be achieved if these ordinary homes have been appropriately

[1] White Paper, *Caring for People* (1989).
[2] White Paper, *Valuing People* (2001).

and well designed. The solutions will not be the same for everyone; some have special requirements, others do not; some will have their own front door, others will share their accommodation with other residents and staff.

The purpose of this guide is to bring together information, experience, case study material and theory to guide building design or adaptation for people with learning disabilities and/or autistic spectrum disorders, and to see what lessons can be learnt from recent practice. The process of planning and designing a service will be described to show how professional consultants, service users, commissioners and managers each contribute to the commissioning and design process, including:

- identifying residents and their particular needs and involving them in the process, to give as much choice as possible;
- being clear about the management and structure for support, skills development and opportunities for relationships and friendship;
- designing for 'ordinary homes' which are located in a community with access to neighbourhood services but suiting special needs as necessary.

The guide includes:

- the 2001 White Paper and other guidance, describing trends in service development;
- an understanding of the variety of needs of people with learning disabilities;
- a framework of options to guide the planning process;
- developing the brief and managing the process of development;
- the special design solutions for special needs;
- case study illustrations and their successes and weaknesses;
- the lessons drawn from these for good design practice.

2. Learning disabilities, policy, needs and services

The stated objectives of the 1998 White Paper, *Modernising Social Services,* were:

> to promote the independence of adults assessed as needing social care support arranged by the local authority, respecting their dignity and furthering their social and economic participation, to enable adults assessed as needing social care support to live as safe, full and as normal a life as possible, in their own home wherever feasible.

2.1 Changes since 1971

Thirty years ago the last White Paper[1] on learning disability services, *Better Services for the Mentally Handicapped,* was published. Prior to this, people had been placed in long-stay institutions detained under the Mental Health Acts. By the end of the 1960s it had become clear that the quality of care in long-stay hospitals was often extremely poor, and that change was needed. The Education Act 1970 ensured that education should be provided for all children, no matter how severe their disability.

The 1971 White Paper gave aims for the next two decades to reduce the number of places in hospitals and increasing provision in the community. It committed the Government to helping people with learning disabilities to live 'as normal a life' as possible, without unnecessary segregation from the community. It emphasised the importance of close collaboration between health, social services and other local agencies.

In 1971 the Government recognised that achieving change would require sustained action, and the White Paper set national targets (for England and Wales) for development of services. These included reducing the number of long-stay hospital places for adults from 52,000 to 27,000 and

[1] White Paper, *Better Services for the Mentally Handicapped* (1971)

increasing the number of residential care places in the community from 4,000 to nearly 30,000.

Many of the aims of the 1971 White Paper have been achieved. Very few large institutions remain and there are no children in long-stay hospitals. Services in the community have expanded and developed. This concentration on reducing the use of hospital services has been beneficial but there is still strong evidence of the need for services and the attention has now turned to the very large number of people with learning disabilities living at home with their families.

In 1969, there were 58,850 patients in NHS hospitals or units and 4,900 places in residential care homes. Today the number of NHS places is less than 10,000 and very few of those in old long-stay hospitals. In contrast there are 53,320 places in residential care in England as at March 2001.

2.2 The aims in 2002

The 2001 White Paper, *Valuing People,* sets out clearly that there is a new agenda.

> People with learning disabilities are amongst the most socially excluded and vulnerable groups in Britain today. Very few have jobs, live in their own homes or have real choice over who cares for them. Many have few friends outside their families and those paid to care for them. Their voices are rarely heard in public. This needs to change.

This is an agenda based on social inclusion, civil rights, choice and independence, the right to be full member of the society in which you live, to choose where you live and to be as independent as you wish to be. The Government also see the new priority as being the substantial number of people with learning disabilities living with carers who will at some time want a home of their own.

> Most people with learning disabilities live with their families. Often they leave the family home only as the result of a crisis such as the

illness or death of the carer. Planning ahead to move to more independent living is not always possible as the appropriate housing, care and support options may not be available. With growing numbers of people living with older carers, the Government wishes to see better forward planning by local councils so that carers do not face continuing uncertainty in old age and their sons and daughters gain greater independence in a planned way.

The 2001 White Paper recognises for the first time the importance of housing – it has never before appeared in learning disability guidance. There is a new radical attitude which accepts that people with learning disabilities can live successfully in different types of housing – from individual self-contained properties, housing networks, group homes, and shared accommodation schemes, through to village and other forms of intentional community, with a full range of tenures, including home ownership. The Department of Health and the Office of the Deputy Prime Minister will be issuing guidance on developing housing and support options and a local housing strategy.

2.3 What is learning disability?

Valuing People is based on the premise that people with learning disabilities are people first. The approach focuses throughout on what people can do, with support where necessary, rather than on what they cannot do.

Learning disability includes the presence of:

- a significantly reduced ability to understand new or complex information, to learn new skills (impaired intelligence); with
- reduced ability to cope independently (impaired social functioning);
- which started before adulthood, with a lasting effect on development.

This definition encompasses people with a broad range of disabilities: an IQ below 70 is not, of itself, a sufficient reason for deciding whether an individual should be provided with additional health and social care support. Many people with learning disabilities also have physical and/or sensory impairments. The definition covers adults with autism who also have learning disabilities, but not those with a higher level autistic spectrum disorder who may be of average or even above average intelligence, such as some people with Asperger's Syndrome. 'Learning disability' does not include all those who have a 'learning difficulty' which is more broadly defined in education legislation.

2.4 How many people have learning disabilities?

The 2001 White Paper quotes rather conservative figures for the population of adults with severe learning disabilities:

> In the case of people with severe and profound learning disabilities, we estimate there are about 120,000 adults of working age and 25,000 older people. In the case of people with mild/moderate learning disabilities, lower estimates suggest a prevalence rate of around 25 per 1000 population – some 1.2 million people in England.
>
> Prevalence of severe and profound learning disability is fairly uniformly distributed across the country and across socio-economic groups. Mild to moderate learning disability, however, has a link to poverty and rates are higher in deprived and urban areas. The number of people with severe and profound learning disabilities in some areas is affected by past funding and placement practices, especially the presence of old long-stay patients and people placed outside their original area of residence by funding authorities.

The White Paper figure for adults with severe learning disability corresponds to a prevalence of 0.25 per cent of the total population.

The Sheffield Case Register is based on those 'with a severe learning disability and expected to need support from community services'. It shows an overall level of 0.45 per cent for adults and children with severe learning disability.[2]

[2] R. Parrott *et al*, *Future Demand for Residential Provision for People with Learning Disabilities*, Manchester, Hester Adrian Research Centre (1997).

The *Joint Investment Plans (JIP) Workbook* recommended current 'administrative prevalence' for adult services is estimated at around five people with learning disabilities per 1,000 general population.[3] This JIP figure (0.5 per cent) for adults is therefore considerably higher than the Sheffield Case Register, which includes children as well.

Using also the case registers of two local authorities who have kept records over time, their figures and the Sheffield study suggest that a prevalence rate of 0.4 per cent adults with severe learning disability in the total population is closer to experience from local authority records and should be used for population estimates.

The rate of 2.5 per cent could be used for mild or moderate disability in the general population. But the *JIP Workbook* goes on to say:

> The learning disability population is likely to continue to increase over the coming years as a result of both the increased life expectancy of people with learning disabilities and the improved medical technology which is resulting in an increase in survival of babies with severe disabilities. Whilst improved screening techniques are leading to a slight reduction in the percentage of births of children with conditions such as Down's Syndrome, this is more than offset by other risk factors, such as the increasing age of mothers at birth.

2.5 Additional or special needs

As we have said above, it is important to understand the wide range of difference there is between people broadly said to have learning disabilities. These are some of the issues identified in the research review *Learning Disabilities: The Fundamental Facts*:[4]

- people with learning disabilities have special health care needs and are more likely to experience certain problems. It can be difficult for

[3] Health and Social Care Joint Unit, *Joint Investment Plan, a Learning Disability Workbook*, Department of Health (2000).
[4] Foundation for People with Learning Disabilities, *Learning Disabilities: The Fundamental Facts* (2001).

them to describe symptoms and there is a high level of unrecognised illness;
- sensory impairment is far more common than in the general population, with 48 per cent having at least a moderate impairment.[5] Hearing loss and visual impairment have both been estimated at 40 per cent of people with severe learning disability;
- physical disability, such as cerebral palsy or other motor impairments occur in 20 to 30 per cent of people with severe learning disability;
- epilepsy is more common than in the general population (between 18 to 32 per cent), with incidence increasing with the severity of disability;
- communication difficulties are common, occurring in between 50 and 90 per cent of people with severe learning disability according to the measures used;
- challenging behaviour, aggression or self injury is identified among people with learning disability and there is research on the effectiveness of behavioural approaches and medication;
- mental health problems have been identified among 25 to 40 per cent of people with learning disability. Both dementia and Alzheimer's disease are relatively common among people with Down's Syndrome.

2.6 Autistic spectrum disorders

Autism and Asperger's Syndrome are now thought by some to describe different parts of a continuum of the same autistic spectrum.[6] The common problems, which may accompany quite different levels of IQ, range from normal to levels characterised by severe or moderate learning disability. Kanner identified autism in 1943 as being associated with:

- lack of emotional contact;
- repetitive routine behaviour;

[5] OPCS, *The Prevalence of Disability in Great Britain,* London, HMSO (1989).
[6] L. Wing, *The Autistic Spectrum: A Guide for Parents and Professionals,* Constable (1996).

- abnormality of speech;
- special visual and memory skills.

Asperger at about the same time described:

- inappropriate social behaviour;
- circumscribed interests;
- awkwardness of speech;
- lack of common sense and specific learning disabilities.

Although diagnosis of Asperger's Syndrome is usually applied to those with an IQ in the more normal range, nevertheless, the problems over communication, understanding and social behaviour create difficulties in managing independence or ordinary everyday living.

The numbers identified as suffering from autism have been increasing and whether this is due to greater awareness and diagnosis or to increasing incidence (the number of new cases) is the subject of continuing investigation and debate. Estimates of prevalence rates (the number in a population) of autistic spectrum disorders among children with special needs has been reported to be about 20 children in 10,000.[7] In 1993 a study in Sweden identified numbers of children with an IQ over 70 with Aspergers Syndrome to be 36 in 10,000.[8] The estimates of numbers requiring a service given below are based on those with severe learning disabilities and do not include those with moderate learning disabilities or higher functioning autism.

2.7 The numbers requiring a service

For housing with care and support, the number requiring a service depends on assessments of needs by social service departments. It will rest on assumptions about how long people may remain in their family

[7] Wing L. and Gould J. (1979), *Severe impairments of social interaction*, Journal of Autism and Development Disorders, 9.
[8] Ehlers S. and Gillberg C. (1993), *The Epidemiology of Asperger's syndrome*, Journal of Child Psychiatry and Psychology.

home before a move is needed. The guidance issued by the Department of Health included the following:

> In considering residential needs local authorities will need regularly to assess and review each individual and the capacity and willingness of the family and carers to continue to support the individual and, insofar as resources allow, plan a package of services.[9]

The main impact on the number of service places needed will depend on the average age at which people leave home. Using the population age profile for Sheffield, the numbers aged 40 or over are about 35 per cent of those with learning disability. If each of those receive accommodation and support the number of places required for a general population of 100,000 will be 175.

The same study suggests that the average age of people leaving home is rather less than 40 (when carers are nearly 70) so the required number of places will be greater than 175. The 1971 White Paper proposed that 155 places were needed per 100,000 population,[10] while the All Wales Strategy proposed a figure of 185 per 100,000[11] – either side of our age 40+ group number.

The gap between services and need has been calculated in several ways. Using a total number required nationally and comparing this with the number of health and social care places available a shortfall of about 27,000 is estimated. Another comparison using a demand and supply model of needs and places available produced a figure of 25,000 places required in England, approximately 50 per 100,000 of the total population.[12]

Besides these estimates of a shortfall between need and places provided for, there is an inevitable turnover in services as people get older. This

[9] Department of Health, *Social Care for Adults with Learning Disabilities,* LAC (92)15 (1992).
[10] White Paper, *Better Services for the Mentally Handicapped* (1971).
[11] *All Wales Strategy,* Welsh Office (1983).
[12] L. Watson and M. Harker, *Community Care Planning: A Model of Housing Needs Assessment,* NFHA.CIOH (1993).

should give the minimum level of annual places provided to keep pace with ageing. Using the general learning disability population figures this should allow for a turnover of ten places a year per 100,000 population – a baseline minimum.

Evidence suggests that the number of people with severe learning disabilities may increase by around 1 per cent per annum for the next 15 years as a result of:

- increased life expectancy, especially among people with Down's Syndrome;
- growing numbers of children and young people with complex and multiple disabilities who now survive into adulthood;
- a sharp rise in the reported numbers of school age children with autistic spectrum disorders, some of whom will have learning disabilities;
- greater prevalence among some minority ethnic populations of South Asian origin (see n2 above).

2.8 Implementing the White Paper recommendations

In order to offer people with learning disabilities greater choice over where and how they live, local councils, the NHS and local housing authorities through the JIP process should work together with people with learning disabilities, carers and service providers to:

- review the range and pattern of current housing, care and support provision;
- plan how to expand choice for individuals, including in particular how to achieve an appropriate mix of different housing, care and support service options locally.

People with learning disabilities should be given a genuine opportunity to choose between housing, care and support options. Councils should respect the preferences of individuals and their families, wherever the preferred options will meet individuals' assessed needs and are affordable.

Local councils and the NHS should co-ordinate their planning, commissioning and funding of care and support services with local housing authorities' work to develop local housing strategies, prepare housing investment plans, devise choice-based lettings systems, develop housing advice services and improve home adaptation services.

Boards should recommend a local housing strategy for people with learning disabilities and related plans for the future commissioning of care and support services by winter 2003. This should be carried out within the context of the housing investment plans.

Learning Disability Partnership Boards will be expected to ensure that they set out plans for the provision of information, advice and advocacy services covering the different aspects of individuals needs, including housing, as part of the Learning Disability Joint Investment Plan (JIP). The new arrangements for *Supporting People* and regulation of care standards are also important and are referred to below.

The 2001 White Paper, *Valuing People*, asks housing and social services to work together to expand housing, care and support options including the following:

- the Learning Disability Development Fund will prioritise 'supported living' approaches for people living with older carers;
- also a priority for the Learning Disability Development Fund will be enabling people living in the remaining long-stay hospitals to move to more appropriate accommodation by 2004.

Among the options identified are supported living: designing services round the particular needs and wishes of individuals rather than congregate living. Small scale ordinary housing is likely to lead to better outcomes across a range of factors than is large housing or hostel provision.

3. Options for living

The 2001 White Paper, *Valuing People,* focuses on expanding choice for individuals, including in particular the issue of how to achieve an appropriate mix of different housing, care and support service options.

3.1 Variety and networks

The present form of services has developed over time to meet various priorities and purposes. The predominant form is registered residential care. The requirement to register services as residential care and minimum requirements for registered homes tends to standardise this form of service. A lack of variety is apparent and there are often gaps, for example for high support complex needs and low support services for more able people.

The overall number of residential care placements recorded represents 70 per cent of services. The number of supported housing placements is not recorded nationally but local surveys show that only 7 or 8 per cent[1] of people with learning disabilities have their own home. There is a lack of self-contained housing options, limited access to tenancies in ordinary housing with support, too many crisis moves from family homes and lack of information about housing out of district.

Care managers and commissioners recognise the need for a better range in supply and in the match of need and type of service. Quite able people remain in shared residential care when they could live more independently. People with high and complex needs are sent out of area because there is nothing suitable in the locality. The lack of variety suggests that the existing and planned services should be looked at together to plan greater diversity. The exercise of choice requires that there are options from which to choose but care managers are keenly

[1] M. Harker and N. King, *An Ordinary Home*, London, LGA (1999).

aware of the narrow base for services and the importance of widening the range available.

People make progress through informed professional contact but there is a lack of information about housing and support. Systems do not encourage non-crisis moves and eligibility criteria gave low priority to non-urgent cases. Housing departments often find the 'care needs' cases awkward and operational liaison is poor.

The traditional form of organisation is a single management structure for a residential home. For diversity, economy of management and flexibility, the single management structure should be extended to include a deliberate range of forms in a locality: a network of housing and services. For reasons of cost, providers often limit themselves to a single product whereas variety is what is wanted.

Twenty-four-hour cover could extend from a group service to self contained tenancies; the community network could include a core house, single site clusters and dispersed locations. Instead of the form of housing suggesting the management structure, management needs to be fitted around a variety of housing forms. This is now increasingly seen as a successful model and in order to develop it has to be planned with provider partners.

3.2 Classification of types of housing

What has been apparent in housing and support for people with learning disabilities over the last 20 years is growing diversity. Past provision was largely based on hospital, large residential care homes or living at home being looked after by parents. There is now more choice and a preference for less institutional settings.

Provision can for simplicity be reduced to two dimensions; form of housing and nature of support. Gradually more 'possibilities' have been added to each dimension; more points have appeared on the continuum of care and housing. This is illustrated in Figure 3.1. Movement from bottom

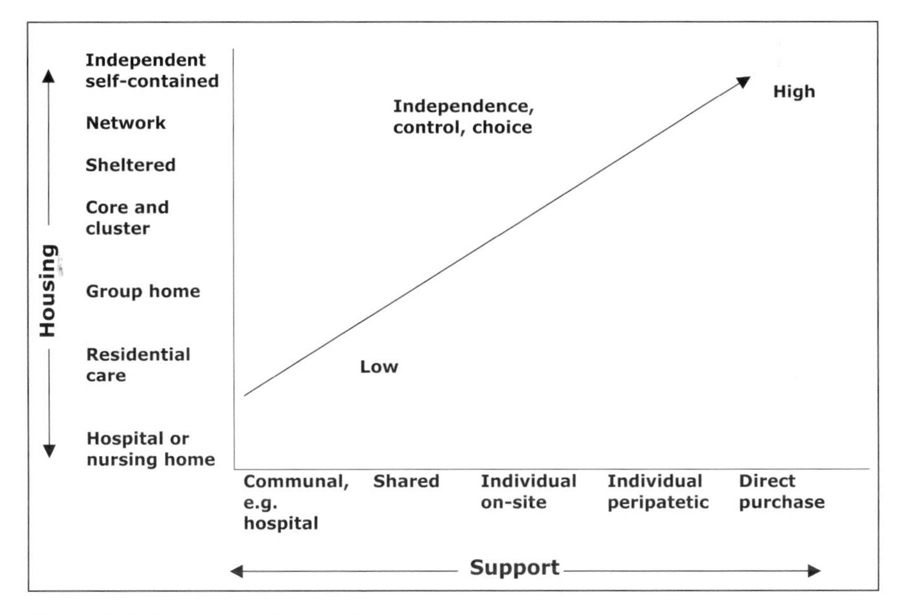

Figure 3.1 Continuum of care and housing

left to top right tends to increase the individual's independence, choice and personal control. The types of accommodation or support identified on each axis are for illustration only (it is not a comprehensive list).

Applying the variables listed in Figure 3.1 there are six main types of housing. These divide into further sub-categories and much of the focus below will be on how different possibilities can be developed in the housing types that provide self-contained accommodation.

Housing is only one dimension of a support service and it is increasingly possible to 'pick and mix' different combinations of the variables outlined above so a service is designed for an individual. Lynn Watson provides an approach to this in *Pick and Mix* (see Table 3.1).[2]

Housing and support alternatives are created by combining a number of variables in different ways. The mix gives the service its defining

[2] L. Watson and M. Tarpey, *Pick and Mix, Developing Flexible Housing Choices in Community Care,* Chartered Institute of Housing (1998).

Table 3.1 Housing and support services

Pick and mix – Select your types				
Housing type	**Support type**	**Support level**	**Management and finances**	**Tenure**
Self-contained independent	Individual service package	High/intensive long term	User managed with direct payments	Mixed owned and rented/owned
Locality/area network	Visiting designated team/worker	Low/medium long term	Grant funded or block purchasing	Rented – local authority
Single site cluster	Adjacent/on-site staff	High/intensive fluctuating	Service charge/ tenant contributions	Rented – housing association
Small shared (2/3 people)	Integral staff night/sleep in	Medium/high increasing	Individual care packages	Mix rented private/ social housing
Large shared (4+ people)	Integral staff Day/office base	High/intensive reducing	Voluntary/ private residential home fees	Licence – stat/ voluntary/ private care agency
Placement/ lodgings	Live-in carer/ support worker	Low/medium reducing	Statutory run and financed service	Rented – private landlord

characteristics. Set out below are the variables which show the many options possible and the effect of different combinations.

3.2.1 Types of built form

These are:

- small or large shared house with common facilities, e.g. registered care home, unregistered group home;
- small or large grouped self-contained units, e.g. sheltered housing, cluster;
- self-contained house or flat, ordinary street property.

There can be degrees of sharing, for example a cluster of self-contained flatlets may share an additional lounge or facilities in a nearby 'core' building. It is also important to identify the need for single storey building, e.g. ordinary bungalow, ground floor access, or very large, purpose built and shared.

3.2.2 Forms of support

These are:

- integral where staff have an office and/or sleep in;
- on-site but not sharing the accommodation, e.g. warden in sheltered scheme;
- peripatetic where staff are based elsewhere and visit;
- mutual support, e.g. as part of a network.

Support may be provided:

- for an individual;
- to be shared with others;
- through an individual or staff team;
- informally by a relative (family carers may resent the title 'informal');
- by a volunteer, e.g. as part of a befriending service;
- by formal, paid support, through employed staff.

The support provider may be:

- employed directly by social services or an NHS Trust;
- employed by a care provider or a housing provider; these may be profit-making companies or charitable organisations;
- employed directly or indirectly by the service user.

3.2.3 Tenure: ownership or renting

This is important, because it determines the rights and security of the occupier and will affect their benefits and income.

(i) Renting

- Licence – common in registered accommodation;
- Secure tenancy – given by a local authority landlord;
- Ordinary assured tenancy – granted by a registered social landlord and sometimes by a private landlord;
- Assured shorthold – granted by a registered social landlord;
- Private renting – assured shorthold commonly granted by private landlord.

(ii) Ownership

- Outright ownership;
- Joint ownership – with one or more others;
- Shared ownership – the occupier owns only part of the equity; the other part is usually owned by the landlord;
- Trust ownership on behalf of beneficiary;
- Limited company.

3.2.4 Registration

Registration as an establishment providing residential care or domiciliary services is important. It can affect quality, security of residence, service culture, homeliness, freedom, choice and control of resident's home and lifestyle, and costs.

3.2.5 Sources of housing

These include:

- local authorities;
- registered social landlords (previously called housing associations);
- private landlords;
- a family home;
- purchase on the open market.

The latter two sources are particularly important in opening up new options, as ultimately someone with a learning disability may directly own property via inheritance or indirectly through a receiver, trust or similar mechanism.

In recent years the possibilities have been considerably extended by recognising many people can live well (or better) in their own, standard (or adapted/purpose built) houses and flats with a suitable care or support package. Such properties may be owned or rented.

(i) Renting

Local Authority: the main source of public sector rented housing. Choice may be limited and there is a chance that individuals may be offered unsuitable housing. However it is a secure tenancy and can be a 'right to succession' property, so that parents who are tenants can pass on property to their children.

Housing Association: the main source of new quasi-public sector rented property, smaller estates/ordinary housing. Some housing associations specialise in accommodating disabled people. An ordinary assured tenancy is normally granted which is fairly secure.

Private Landlord: a less secure form of assured shorthold tenancy (its biggest disadvantage), some landlords may refuse to let property to people on benefits. However, it extends the choice of property.

Renting from parents/relatives: it is possible for parents to acquire a property, which is then rented to a son/daughter. Provided the arrangements are established for good reasons, not simply to access benefits, and the letting is on a commercial basis the disabled person should qualify for Housing Benefit (if eligible). Housing Benefit will therefore contribute to repaying a mortgage. The attractions of this route are the extra choice, control and security.[3]

The risk is that the parents will be treated as private landlords, resulting in the rent set by the rent officer, on which Housing Benefit is paid not fully meeting the costs of loan repayments and management and maintenance. Increasingly families making long term financial provision for disabled children set up discretionary trusts. It is possible for property held in such a trust to be rented to beneficiaries of the trust. The same restrictions that apply to parents renting directly apply to discretionary trusts.

Taking over a tenancy: adult children may take over the tenancy of the parents' property so that they can continue to live in the family home where this is the best option. The possibilities are:

- to succeed to a tenancy – this depends on the type of landlord and if the relatives had themselves succeeded;
- to become a joint tenant – a good way of ensuring continuity; or
- to ask the landlord to grant a new tenancy.

(ii) Owning

Around three out of four parents of adults with a learning disability are home owners. Parents of retirement age mostly own property outright. In some circumstances it may make sense to plan around the son/daughter continuing to live in the family home, possibly sharing with one or two other people. The advantages can be to stay in a familiar property and

[3] For more details on Housing Benefit regulations applying to parents or trust see Statutory Instrument No 3257 (1998).

neighbourhood where the person may be known in the community and have friends.

Inheritance: the normal way of passing on property. The disadvantages are how management and maintenance are arranged, a risk the local authority will put a legal charge on the property to recover costs of care when it is eventually sold and problems of dividing up the family estate between other siblings who should also inherit.

Trust: rather than direct inheritance, property may be placed in trust. This should avoid the risk of a local authority recovering charges and provides a mechanism for managing and maintaining the property via the trustees. The trustees can contract with an agency for this work if they do not wish to do it themselves.

Disposal to a third party: the property may be sold to another organisation (or individual) on the condition the son or daughter continues to live in the property as long as it remains suitable. The problem is finding anyone willing to buy and if they are the very low valuation placed on the (tenanted) property.

Gift: occasionally parents or relatives gift a property to a charity or housing association subject to similar conditions to those above. Difficulties most usually arise over conditions placed on the gift and certainty/ability of the receiving body to meet the conditions.

Lease: a variant on gift of outright disposal is to grant a lease for a period like 21 years to an organisation (usually a housing association). The relatives get a capital payment (or income) although this will be much less than the open market, freehold value, without a tenant. On expiry of the lease the property can revert to a trust or be disposed of and proceeds distributed amongst other members of the family if the property is no longer required.[4]

[4] Details of these and other possibilities are set out in N. King, *Family Homes,* Mental Health Foundation (2001).

A second possibility is for the disabled person to buy their own home. There are several ways this can be arranged.

Outright purchase: occasionally relatives are in a position to buy a property. As explained above if this has to be purchased with a mortgage Housing Benefit may be available to pay a rent and to offset some of the repayments. Other people may share the property and also pay a rent.

Shared ownership: shared ownership is where an individual buys part of a property (25%, 50%, 75%) and rents the other part from the landlord usually a housing association. This enables people who could not otherwise afford to buy to gain all the benefits of ownership like security of tenure and ability to choose a property on the open market.

The rented part will be eligible for Housing Benefit if the person qualifies and the rent can include management and maintenance costs if the lease puts this obligation on the landlord.

The part which is purchased may be bought by relatives, from an individual's own resources (e.g. an inheritance or capital built up while in hospital) or through a mortgage. There are special income support regulations that apply to some disabled people to repay a loan (see below).

Joint ownership: up to four people may combine resources to jointly purchase property. This may be four disabled people, but more commonly a relative will buy a property jointly with a disabled person.

Group purchase: sometimes families want to combine together to buy a property for relatives to share. This is perfectly possible and there are a number of arrangements. One possibility, where the number of families is large, is to set up a company in which the families are shareholders. The company is a legal entity, which can therefore borrow, develop, manage and maintain the property.

(iii) Income Support Mortgage Interest Payments (ISMI)

For disabled people eligible for income support there are special provision within the Income Support Regulations that can be used to repay the interest on a mortgage. This is relevant where the person needs, "alternative accommodation more suited to their special needs as a disabled person."[5] This provision has been particularly successful when used by disabled people becoming shared owners. ISMI will only repay interest not capital so it is usual to take out an interest only mortgage. Not all mortgage providers will lend to people on Income Support and sometimes questions about legal capacity prevent a mortgage being taken out.[6]

3.2.6 Design and adaptation

This includes:

- property purpose built and designed specifically for people with complex needs, physical or sensory impairment;
- ordinary property but no adaptation is required for the individual concerned;
- property that can be made acceptable through adaptations.

Disabled facilities grants (DFG) and other grants are available to adapt privately rented or owned properties. In certain circumstances for a disabled person who qualifies, DFGs are mandatory – the authority has to make a grant. Local authority properties are usually dealt with by the council with funding from the Housing Revenue Account. It is possible to use DFG to adapt a council property but it is rare in practice. Minor adaptations and aids are available through social services to all, usually following an assessment by an occupational therapist. The Social Fund can sometimes contribute to costs of aids or adaptations or special equipment.

[5] General Income and Support Regulations, Schedule 2, Para 4, sub-para 9.
[6] For more details on home ownership and Income Support provision see N. King *Ownership Options,* National Housing Federation (1996). On housing choices in general see N. King and M. Harker, *Making Housing Choices,* Pavilion (2000).

3.2.7 Purchase of service

This may be:

- funded wholly by the local authority as residential care and contracted through a provider or provided directly;
- funded by the local authority contributing toward the cost of support or domiciliary care;
- wholly funded by the NHS as a health service where the resident is still technically an 'in patient';
- funded by the NHS as social care (under a 'section 28a arrangement' for people resettled from hospital);
- purchased by the service user (or on their behalf by an advocate/carer) using either ILF (independent living fund) or direct payments or income support and housing benefits;
- paid through supported housing management grant to a housing association or in due course a new specific grant for support to come into being in 2003;
- paid for by 'preserved rights' entitlement to residential care benefits;
- some combination of the above.

3.3 Six main types

The six main types of housing available are set out in Table 3.2 along with sub-types. This is, however, a simplification: a key message from spelling out all the variables that can be combined to create a service is that there are literally hundreds of possibilities. This is also the point of the 'Pick and Mix' idea.

Many of these individual types can be managed through a network or locality service using a mix of building or tenure/ownership types within a single support service.

Table 3.2: Main types of housing available

Type	Sub-type examples
Self-contained independent housing Self-contained accommodation usually unregistered, various forms of care and support are possible including management within a locality service.	Full and joint ownership Shared ownership Trust ownership Rented from local authority, private or registered social landlord Rented from parents Sub-letting and lodgers
Locality based Properties grouped in a small geographical area, self-contained or shared. A central resource, which can be shared facilities and/or staff can be used by all the residents. Accommodation is usually rented and may be registered but more often unregistered. Staff do not live in resident's own accommodation.	Core and cluster Community support network Mixed shared and self-contained
Single site self-contained or shared housing Larger scale building with a number of self-contained flats or bedsits or shared properties. Staff on site and some shared facilities in the building such as launderette, lounge, games room and office or sleep-in facilities for staff.	Cluster flats or bedsits Sheltered housing Mixed shared and self-contained

Table 3.2: Main types of housing available – *continued*

Type	Sub-type examples
Small shared housing Less than four people, registered or unregistered. Characteristic is shared living and shared facilities. Although there may be some private facilities, e.g. cooker, en-suite bathroom, it is not fully self-contained accommodation. Staff may be visiting or permanently on site.	Small registered care home Group home – unregistered
Large shared housing Four or more people live together. Few private facilities. Usually registered with on-site, paid staff with someone on duty up to 24 hours a day.	Large registered care home
Individual placement Individual lives with family who provide accommodation and support in ordinary housing.	Adult family placement Supported lodging

3.4 Cost and quality

A substantial study and report was published for the Department of Health[7] looking at the cost and quality of different forms of residential and supported housing services.

[7] E. Emerson et *al*, *Quality and Cost of Residential Supports for People with Learning Disabilities, Summary Report*, Manchester, Hester Adrian Research Centre (1996).

Larger residential care homes are still common although those provided by local authorities 20 years ago of 15 to 25 places are now few in number. Research evidence on the quality and costs of hostels suggests they serve less well than ordinary small scale housing in terms of user satisfaction, material and social environment, privacy and choice, participation in domestic activities and staff support.[8]

Small scale ordinary housing has grown as a form of service and demonstrated better outcomes than long-stay hospitals and hostels, and have been successfully used for people with severe or profound learning disabilities, challenging behaviour and complex and multiple disabilities. Costs vary widely for each type of service but small scale ordinary housing services do appear to be marginally more expensive than larger scale alternatives.

However, research evidence also indicates that, while small-scale ordinary housing may be a preferred option, outcomes do not match up against the usual standards of living: choice over where to live and who to live with, meaningful friendships, avoidance of poverty, employment and healthy lifestyles.

Supported housing or supported living is where people have their own home and more individualised support services. This should give proper rights of occupancy, more individual choice and support arrangements. The costs of supported living schemes appear to be marginally higher than the costs of ordinary housing schemes and hostels.

Independent living schemes for relatively able people with learning disabilities have been thoroughly evaluated in one study,[9] which demonstrated that the positive and valued aspects of independent living were often accompanied by poverty, unemployment and victimisation by people in local communities. If supported housing is not to suffer the

[8] E. Emerson *et al*, *Residential Provision for People with Learning Disabilities, Summary Report*, Manchester, Hester Adrian Research Centre (1996).
[9] M. Flynn, *Independent Living for Adults with Mental Handicap*, London, Cassells (1989).

same criticism, the quality of the support for residents has to be adequately provided and supervised.

These different types may be structured and designed with different aims. Quality outcomes are probably most importantly linked with good management and staff practices such as 'active support' based on individual plans, good communication skills, more time spent on residents' needs and activities, and monitoring specific planned outcomes.

3.5 What do we want from housing and support services?

In work with a group of local authorities recently in the North West of England[10] these were their aims for a housing and support service:

- the service should provide what the person says they want: 'a home of their own', 'an ordinary or special home', 'your own front door key';
- it should meet their essential needs, specifying desired outcomes or results;
- a general aim may be to promote independence, choice and participation in daily living, social and daytime activities, employment opportunities;
- these should be framed in an individual care plan, which will be regularly reviewed to see what is achieved and how it may change;
- the flexibility of a care plan should allow for change in the type or hours of support given and for opportunity to move;
- there should be a clear statement of what the service aims are: standards, targets or outcomes either generally or in respect of individuals and how they will be consistently achieved;

[10] NW Development Group Programme, *Housing and Support Partnership* (2001).

- the results or outcomes to be achieved should in some way be measurable so that personal benefits, development or progress can be confidently identified;
- the service should also be assessed against what it has said it will achieve through a transparent evaluation process such as that offered through accreditation programmes;
- the service should be able to demonstrate value for money using best value or cost effectiveness measures to make comparison between services on the basis of the stated aims;
- standards – expected measures of performance – should include minimum standards of accommodation, amenity and management;
- residents should have a proper occupancy agreement, a tenancy agreement and support agreement. The terms of occupation should take account of residents' disposable income, the use of direct payments and any charges made for services;
- management standards should include staffing which gives a resident a named person with particular responsibility and knowledge of their needs and wishes.

In Chapter 5, the guide looks particularly at the matter of standards of accommodation.

3.6 Registered care

Government policy for community care aims to promote independence while protecting service users' safety. The new regulatory framework under the Care Standards Act 2000 aims to ensure high standards of care and to protect vulnerable people, but the Act will not fundamentally change the definition of a residential care home as compared with the current legislation.

The Registered Homes Act 1984 provided for registration of establishments providing personal or nursing care. From 2002 an establishment providing residential accommodation together with nursing or personal care has to register under the Care Standards Act 2000 which replaced the Registered Homes Act 1984.

The reasons that a decision about registration is important are that:

- there are wide and enforceable responsibilities for the care, welfare and supervision of residents and for standards of the accommodation;
- residents' personal income is limited and housing benefit is not payable in a registered home;
- registration can create an institutional environment and add to costs;
- it sets minimum standards but can create inflexibilities.

The Act also introduces a new form of support, which is registerable. This is the carrying on of a domiciliary care agency. If a registered social landlord or voluntary organisation arranges for people in their homes to receive personal care it will need to be registered.

One of the most fundamental changes to be introduced by the 2000 Act is the introduction of a new authority to regulate registration. Under the 1984 Act the registration authority has been a local inspectorate unit run by the local social services authority for the area in which the home is situated. Once the 2000 Act becomes law the registration of all care homes will be dealt with and regulated by the National Care Standards Commission instead of local units.

The current legal opinion is that a tenancy with care does not fall under the Registered Homes Act, and registration and inspection units have usually taken the view that if a tenancy has been issued then the premises should not be registered as it would interfere with tenancy rights.

A government minister's advice during the passage of the Care Standards Act 2000 through Parliament reflects this too. 'Where care is provided to people in their own home – whether as owner occupier or tenant – that home will not be registerable as a care home' and 'it is immaterial whether the person is living alone or with others'. In such cases if personal care is provided by a domiciliary care agency, the agency but not the home should be registered under the 2000 Act.

Providing 'accommodation together with personal care' suggests the two come as part of a package and there is an argument that housing is better separated contractually from care or support, provided it is properly supervised and if need be regulated as domiciliary care. It allows for an individual's tenancy rights, more non-institutional arrangements and for more independence. The Care Standards Act 2000 provides for the registration and supervision of domiciliary care so the safeguards for residents needing care and support are extended to housing tenancies.

Useful guidance has been given in a consultation paper,[11] which clarifies the following in respect of the requirement for an establishment to be registered:

- personal care means assistance with bodily functions such as feeding, bathing and toileting;
- both accommodation and care should be provided by the establishment;
- the requirement would not apply to someone having a proper tenancy of their own home.

Guidance on the 2000 Act and standards for homes is dealt with in Chapter 5.

3.7 Planning for individuals: a checklist

Key variables defining options are listed in the checklist below to help refine the best options for the circumstances. Not all may be relevant and in some cases any choice may be reasonable.

Type of accommodation required may include:

- **Large scale shared** – accommodation for a group of five or more people, often with similar design features to the small shared model

[11] Department of Health, *Residential Care, Housing Care and Support Schemes and Supporting People* (2001).

but more likely to have a staff sleep-in room and/or office accommodation within the building. Usually registered as care home.

- **Small scale shared** – accommodation for a group of two to four people, normally with individual bedrooms and shared kitchen, bathroom and living rooms. There may be private bathrooms or individual kitchens/cooking facilities. Registered or unregistered.
- **Single site cluster** – grouped units of accommodation, usually but not necessarily purpose-designed or converted, within one building or on a single site. Some schemes will have communal facilities and staff accommodation.
- **Locality/area network** – mainstream housing, usually self-contained but may include small shared flats or houses, linked with other accommodation through a shared support service (e.g. peripatetic or 'floating support'). The service may be attached to a staffed hostel or 'core' house.
- **Self-contained independent** – mainstream housing, rented or owner occupied, where the person is the sole or joint householder. Support is provided on an individualised basis (e.g. community care package or direct payment to purchase care/support).
- **Lodgings/adult placement** – accommodation within the household of someone, normally a non-relative, who has been specifically recruited to provide support on a paid basis. There may be one or several residents within a single household.

Checklist of accommodation options

(i) Accommodation type

- ☐ Registered large (5+)
- ☐ Registered small (-4) group home
- ☐ Shared unregistered group home
- ☐ Single site cluster of self-contained flats
- ☐ Self-contained/own home
- ☐ Adult placement/lodging
- ☐ Other

(ii) Built form

- ☐ House
- ☐ Flat
- ☐ Bungalow
- ☐ Ground floor
- ☐ Adapted or wheelchair accommodation
- ☐ Design and build package/purpose built

(iii) Building separation

- ☐ Does the property need to be separate from neighbouring properties for noise or other reasons?
- ☐ Is proximity to other properties preferable: flat, core and cluster, network, sheltered block or other?

(iv) Source of housing

- ☐ Renting from the local authority
- ☐ Renting from a housing association
- ☐ Renting from private landlord
- ☐ Buying new or existing property

- [ ] Shared ownership
- [ ] Capital available so purchase possible
- [ ] Remaining in family home: inheriting or keeping tenancy
- [ ] Renting from parents/family
- [ ] Joint purchase with other families
- [ ] Property put in a trust
- [ ] Using a charity
- [ ] Other

(v) Living with?

- [ ] Living alone
- [ ] Alone, but near other people
- [ ] With other people
- [ ] With friends
- [ ] With family members
- [ ] In another family
- [ ] With staff in the house
- [ ] With staff nearby
- [ ] With volunteer/support tenant

(vi) Support options

- [ ] Live-in support staff
- [ ] Directly employed carers, e.g. using direct payments/ILF
- [ ] Support tenant/CSV
- [ ] Domiciliary, visiting support staff
- [ ] Community network
- [ ] Additional health care
- [ ] Psychiatric care
- [ ] Advocacy
- [ ] Circle of support
- [ ] Family, friends, informal support network
- [ ] Home help
- [ ] Meals service
- [ ] Other

(vii) Support provider

- ☐ Local authority
- ☐ Health or care trust
- ☐ Independent or voluntary provider
- ☐ Housing association
- ☐ Direct employment
- ☐ Parents/family
- ☐ Other

(viii) Paying for support

- ☐ Purchased by local authority
- ☐ Purchased by local authority and health
- ☐ Direct payments
- ☐ Privately funded
- ☐ Charitable funding
- ☐ Independent living fund
- ☐ Using other benefits/income
- ☐ Other

(ix) Location and amenities

- ☐ Area: town or country
- ☐ Somewhere quiet
- ☐ Somewhere lively
- ☐ Near:
  - __ town centre
  - __ shops
  - __ bus or railway services
  - __ work/college
  - __ family
- ☐ With a garden
- ☐ Plenty of space in the house
- ☐ Other

(x) Facilities, aids and equipment requirements

- ☐ Special aids equipment needed
- ☐ Wheelchair accommodation
- ☐ Hoist
- ☐ Special bath
- ☐ Assistive technology
- ☐ Other

(xi) Any additional special requirements to be taken into account?

- ☐ Floor finishes
- ☐ Internal doors
- ☐ Window openings
- ☐ Glazing
- ☐ Paint and finishes
- ☐ Bathroom fittings
- ☐ Kitchen fittings
- ☐ Kitchen equipment
- ☐ Heating and hot water
- ☐ Lighting
- ☐ Entrance
- ☐ Security
- ☐ External and garden
- ☐ Other

(This might include robust garden furniture, toughened glass, or facilities for hobbies.)

4. Managing the process

In Chapter 3, we have already noted some ideas from service managers and commissioners about what is important for a housing and support service. Producing good solutions either for individuals or for a managed service means understanding individual requirements, knowing what is possible and managing the process of design and development in the best way achievable. This chapter tries to give a summary of the potential and pitfalls.

4.1 Having a choice: the residents' views

There are all kinds of individual wants and needs but some priorities or issues are commonly raised in residents' surveys and research:

- choice of where and who you live with;
- sharing or living alone;
- having a home of your own;
- homeliness of the accommodation;
- location – for reasons of work, friends or family networks;
- living in a good area;
- good physical standards of housing, properly equipped;
- space for belongings;
- choice of furniture and decoration;
- security, freedom from harassment or victimisation;
- support and help with daily living, money management and household;
- accessibility and responsiveness of support staff or services.

The relative importance of different priorities varies and so do the preferences on points of choice. In a small survey[1] carried out for housing association tenants these were some of the key points:

[1] *Design Matters*, New Dimensions Group (unpublished) (1998).

- Location is of great importance to residents. They wanted to be near facilities for transport and work, near pubs, cinema, shops, a library and specialist day facilities.
- Many residents in shared accommodation liked it, especially some younger residents who liked the company. However a number did indicate that in a few years time they would like to be in a flat of their own. When residents were not getting on, they wanted the chance to move.
- Those in self-contained accommodation valued their independence; many had previously shared for many years and really appreciated their own flat or house. They felt it was very hard to adapt and settle initially and they had felt a bit lonely at times. Higher support was needed at the beginning of a tenancy to prevent people failing.
- People in shared accommodation generally felt that larger bedrooms were important as this was their private space. An en-suite bathroom was desirable.
- Fitted wardrobes were disliked if it restricted the furniture layout within the room. Tenants wanted to be able to change their room around.
- A spare room was seen as important in a shared house where a relative or friend could stay overnight without disrupting the house. The spare room could also serve as a second lounge.

Quite clearly residents had some strong views and wanted to be able to express them. More services are being designed around individuals: listening carefully to what individuals say has not always had enough attention. The 2001 White Paper on learning disability emphasises choice and this should have greater weight. Too often people have been fitted into services.

4.2 The views of managers and service commissioners

From discussion with managers and service commissioners, these were some of the key considerations which were identified:

- making the most of ordinary housing and existing stock if it is fit for the purpose and suitable management or support arrangements are proposed; finding the right home for someone may not require a special development or design solution;
- housing development should take account of a range of views of residents, managers, commissioners, regulators, and professional consultants;
- proposals for any project need to be tested as thoroughly as possible with all concerned and competing demands identified;
- residents should be identified at an early stage so that the planning process involves them and includes any special requirements affecting design;
- feedback from other similar projects should be incorporated in the early decision-making.

4.3 First principles for new development

The early structure for planning development should include:

- key principles: aims for ordinary housing, domestic scale and access to community services need to be agreed;
- plans for the type of management and the form of support proposed, the structure for support for residents;
- the mix of dwellings: shared and self-contained housing each have their uses and combinations which take account of management requirements and individual resident preferences are important;
- the balance between communal living and personal space in shared housing and grouped flats;
- regulation and its potential impact on the building design – the likely extent of regulation, particularly planning consent and the need to register as a care home;
- particular design requirements, e.g. for people with physical disabilities or other special needs, should be noted;

- how special does the building have to be and how fit or adaptable for other uses;
- building in adaptability – the Lifetime Homes approach (*see* Chapter 5) – incorporating features which make for flexibility should the needs of residents or the use change.

4.4 A dynamic process

A good building design should take account of the needs of the resident, support and management for the home. The building decisions could be illustrated as shown in Figure 4.1. Beginning with the individual residents, then with the organisation for management and support, the key decisions about buildings can be made.

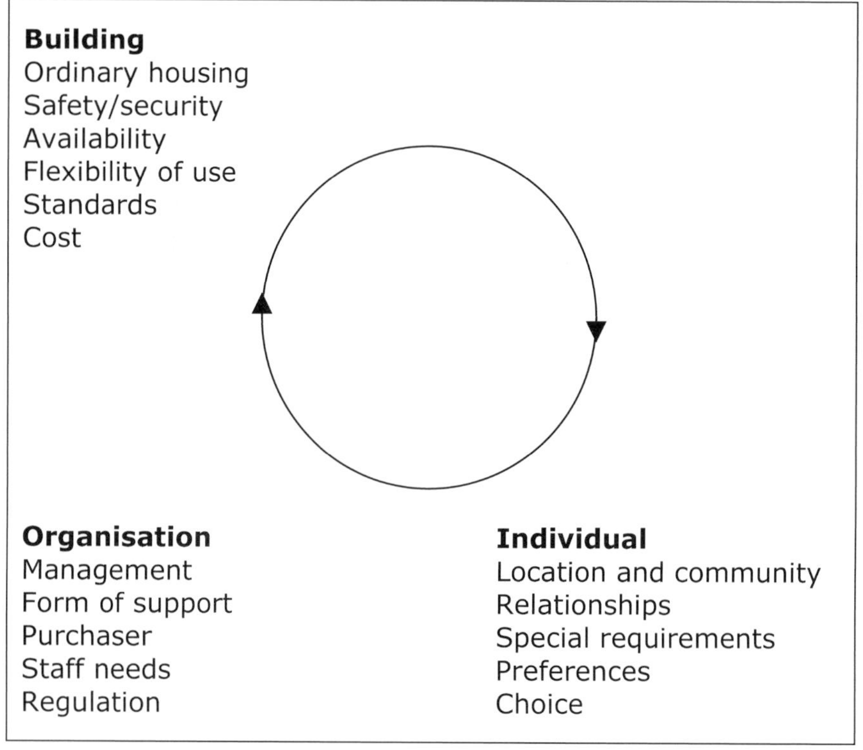

Figure 4.1 Decisions for design

The balance too often has been toward the service needs rather than the resident but the best approach is that projects should be based as closely as possible on individual need and choice, independence and autonomy. Necessarily projects for those with higher support needs will have to take account of organisation and staffing arrangements. The illustration in Figure 3.1 (*see* p. 17) shows the continuum from institutional to individual support arrangements. Assuming it is desirable to give as much individual choice and autonomy as possible, the organisational requirements should be challenged to ensure that the service meets the individual's needs rather than the other way round.

Figure 4.1 suggests different sources for inputs and recognises that there are a range of different possibilities for each. Secondly, it allows that the weight of opinion will vary. Thirdly, it fits with a market approach where the consumers, purchasers and providers meet to work out a solution.

Using the framework in Figure 4.1, the views of the stakeholders (purchasers, providers, regulators) and residents can be compared to see if these form consistent aims for the service that can be achieved through the building. The variety of influence has to be reconciled and for the developer, the building solution also has to be deliverable. Further comments are given below on some of the main considerations.

4.5 Choice of where to live

The location of the site or property is one of the most important considerations in any scheme. It is the first thing most home buyers think about. Accessibility to shops and local facilities, transport links, job opportunities and day centres are essential. Proximity and access to existing family, friends and support networks are likely to be very important for people.

Neither managers nor residents are usually happy about putting services in poor neighbourhoods or areas where there are high levels of multi-occupation. The research by Margaret Flynn was very clear about the risks of harassment and victimisation,[2] but the residents' view about the neighbourhood will be influenced by where they were brought up, and by their own background and interests. Liaison with tenants and other stakeholders direct the location of the accommodation. This should take account of existing family and support networks.

Four important factors are:

- to avoid isolation, geographical or social;
- the importance of friendship and support networks;
- safety, security and freedom from harassment;
- avoiding concentrations of special services and multiple occupation.

The site and outward appearance of the accommodation should not set the building and users apart from the local community.

Travel for residents, staff and their visitors should be straightforward. Public transport should be accessible, nearby and frequent. If possible residents should be able to walk to local shops. There should be space for parking, allowing for staff and visitors. This should not be such that it is too dominant or obtrusive and it can be a problem when making use of ordinary housing.

Hospital sites may be available for development land but for people with a learning disability the use of a hospital site could convey the impression that residents are part of a hospital campus. If a hospital has been demolished then the land may be suitable, but if not, the grounds and surroundings may be stigmatised by the presence of the institution both for the neighbours and those with experience of the institution.

Privacy and some seclusion may be important in selecting a location, site or building. Residents generally will not want to be overlooked every time they use the garden and there may be potential problems of noise or lack of privacy, which need careful attention.

[2] M. Flynn, *Independent Living for Adults with Mental Handicap,* London, Cassells (1989).

4.6 Sharing or not?

Very few people with learning disabilities have their own self-contained accommodation. In a review of six local authorities[3] in 1999, only 7 per cent had their own home.

In Margaret Flynn's study of independent living,[4] nearly one-third lived alone, about the same number with two or more people and the largest group lived with one other person.

In Emerson's study[5] of 281 residents in community-based housing, only 32 were living alone. But when a group of people were asked what they wanted in an examination of demand,[6] more than half wanted their own flat on its own or in a cluster of flats.

Self-contained accommodation was seen as giving more freedom and the benefits of sharing were security, companionship and support. For people moving from hospital or a larger institution, a small, shared house is more homely, but when residents in group homes were asked, about one-third said they would like to live on their own or in their own home with a few friends. Those who wanted their own flat said they wanted to be near their friends but not necessarily living in the same room or flat.

One of the options in our case studies provides an intermediate solution which appears popular if it is available. This is the single site cluster of self-contained flats, such as a small sheltered housing project.

[3] M. Harker and N. King, *An Ordinary Home,* London, LGA (1999).
[4] Flynn, 1989, n 2 above.
[5] E. Emerson *et al, Quality and Cost of Residential Supports for People with Learning Disabilities, Summary Report,* Manchester, Hester Adrian Research Centre (1996).
[6] J. Hudson, L. Watson and G. Allan, *Moving Obstacles: Housing Choices and Community Care,* Policy Press, University of Bristol (1997).

In *Pick and Mix,*[7] Lynn Watson stated that a self-contained cluster scheme for people with high support needs was seen to have the benefits of:

- unobtrusive staff presence;
- easily filled vacancies;
- flexibility for varying support;
- private living space;
- more choice and control by the resident; and
- help to avoid social isolation.

A small scale, high support shared scheme allows the benefits of social contact and support but has problems because of:

- vacancies which cannot easily be filled nor costs covered;
- potential friction between residents;
- single support regime for a range of needs in the group.

4.7 Mixed and cluster schemes

The first assumptions about non-institutional accommodation for people with learning difficulties in 1973 were only of one scale – small, mini institutions of 16 to 25 people, and later on hostels and group homes. The scale followed the expected requirement for an establishment of sufficient size for economical staffing and supervision. The philosophy of the time also allowed for the value of the therapeutic community, an actual benefit of living together, learning skills and social behaviour in a controlled and beneficial environment.

This gave way in the 1980s to greater emphasis on ordinary living and domestic scale accommodation leading to 'core and cluster' schemes, which recognised the possibility of mixing types of accommodation within a network or community and allowed for more efficient use of staff.

[7] L. Watson and M. Tarpey, *Pick and Mix, Developing Flexible Housing Choices in Community Care*, Chartered Institute of Housing (1998).

A planned mix of dwelling types managed as a group can have the same advantages as a 'core and cluster' development:

- using self-contained accommodation and ordinary existing stock;
- fulfilling the aim for small scale domestic buildings;
- fulfilling the need for communities;
- economical staffing arrangements;
- 24-hour or on-call assistance;
- services that are responsive to changing needs;
- giving residents a choice of their own home;
- offering access to 'move on'.

Another form of solution is the 'living support network' which links separate tenancies in a neighbourhood. A mix of separate and shared housing within a group structure allows for flexibility of management and choice for residents.

For residents, managers and commissioners, a wider range or choice can be offered within a safe, well staffed and managed network. Evidence from those simply placed in isolated tenancies shows the threat of isolation, vulnerability and sometimes harassment. The evidence from our case studies reinforces the idea of mixed dwelling types within a single management structure to provide for variety and stability.

4.8 Using existing housing or purpose built

Not all housing needs to be provided through new building. Given the numbers needing accommodation, good use of existing stock is essential. The advantages of ordinary stock are:

- availability and cost;
- flexibility, alternative uses;
- domestic scale;
- not identifiably different;

and for specially designed housing:

- additional allowance for shared occupation;
- more intensive use;
- allows for special physical or other needs;
- provides for on-site staffing;
- potentially higher amenity and space standards.

Existing, improved or converted housing should also have the benefit of an ordinary appearance and an established community but may not lend itself to substantial adaptation, e.g. for physical disabilities.

New build can be produced to suit a variety of demands but it can appear institutional and may not merge into a neighbourhood so readily. New estate locations may also be a problem, with concentrations of low income households and 'instant' communities which are sometimes less tolerant and accepting than more established neighbourhoods.

In order to provide places for people with learning disabilities each of the following are needed:

- new capital funding for those projects which require special design or adaptation;
- improvement or adaptation of existing stock to suit a special need;
- using ordinary stock (which fulfils standards for location and condition) and meeting need through allocation and selection priorities.

4.9 Capital funding

In our earlier discussion of housing types in Chapter 3, different providers were identified: private, charitable, public sector and social landlords. Different funding possibilities apply to each and it is important that these are well understood in an initial appraisal. Funding may influence design: affordability, cost limits for public finance, borrowing rules for private finance, conditions on health and social services grants. Funding is also available for individuals including the following.

Disabled facilities grants (DFG) are available to provide facilities and adaptations to help a disabled person to live independently. The disabled facilities grant is a mandatory grant in specific circumstances. It must be given if a person is disabled and does not have access to their home and to the basic amenities within it, provided that they qualify on income grounds. Local housing authorities administer DFGs. When funding is inadequate authorities may seek to delay advancing the grant although there is a timescale specified. Legal advice is that authorities should not use lack of resources to refuse a mandatory grant.[8] Discretionary grants can be given for a wide range of other work to make a home suitable for a disabled person, e.g. to enable them to get employment.[9]

Shared ownership is an arrangement for part owning and part renting from a housing association. The people who are most likely to find shared ownership helpful are:

- those who have some money but not enough to buy a house outright or those who have some money and a small, regular income;
- those with parents who can put up the capital to help provide a share of a house;
- those with a trust sufficient to purchase part of a property.[10]

Income support for mortgage interest (ISMI) payments,[11] allowed on 'qualifying' loans:

- to purchase an interest in the home;
- to pay for repairs and improvements which are needed to maintain its fitness;

[8] For advice on good practice see *Needs first: a good practice guide for housing associations to practicing tenants' needs for adaptions*, Hodis (2001).
[9] Housing Options Factsheet No 10, *Adapting Property*.
[10] Housing Options Factsheet No 2, *Shared Ownership*.
[11] Housing Options Factsheet No 8, *Income Support for Mortgage Interest*.

- to pay for certain service charges for repairs and improvements;
- to repay a loan which had originally been taken out to purchase an interest in the home or to pay for qualifying repairs or improvements.

Families may have capital or property, which could be used for the benefit of a family member. Discretionary trusts may be used by parents or other relatives as a way of making long term financial provision for a disabled child. The reason a trust is useful is that assets once put in trust do not belong to either the donor parents, 'settlor' in legal terms or the 'object' of the trust (disabled son or daughter who is intended to benefit). A trust may also be used to hold, manage and maintain property.[12]

Charities, local authorities, health trusts, and private providers have each grown in their own way as providers of housing and support services. Registered social landlords have become an important provider of special housing over many years because of their ability to use a variety of funding sources. Funding may come through social housing grant, private finance and from health and social services, as our case studies illustrate.

The Housing Corporation is the recognised channel for public housing grant and local authority support for a project is vital in a bid for funding and for the form of project proposed. The proposals in *Supporting People*[13] also underline the importance to be given to local authority support for services.

The Housing Corporation works against a 'total cost indicator' (TCI) yardstick. This allows capital costs to be directly compared and value for money assessed. Allowance is made for the additional costs of designing for older people, for physical disability and shared housing. However, the building designed for special use to more demanding specifications may compare unfavourably in value for money alongside general needs dwellings and so struggle within this funding system. In our case studies

[12] N. King, *Using Parental Property,* Foundation for People with Learning Disabilities (2001).
[13] Department of Transport, Local Government and the Regions, *Supporting People, Administrative Guidance* (2001).

the use of free land, charitable and local authority grant funding had been used to help. (The capital cost per place ranged between £50,000 – 100,000.)

Social services support for capital bids should inform the housing investment programme. It is important to demonstrate how essential needs are being met, or how special features or higher scheme standards contribute to a long term success. In some cases it can be seen that savings on capital grants may mean higher revenue costs.

Increasing emphasis is being put on using private finance for securing social housing. Accommodation commissioned for care in the community by health authorities has often been funded in this way. There has been recent encouragement to use the government Private Finance Initiative (PFI) for learning disability services but using private finance can mean pushing rent levels higher to recover borrowing costs. This may be manageable in specialist services where a higher rent is still only a small part of annual revenue costs, but it has to be managed carefully where people are on limited benefits or working. The issue of affordability then needs careful assessment.

Several elements are vital for initial funding appraisals:

- well-developed brief as the starting point for estimating the budget for capital costs and valuation of the building produced;
- good understanding of the range of funding sources and the likely conditions to be satisfied to qualify for funding;
- long-term forecast for revenue: income for accommodation, its management and maintenance from rents or fees against the repayments required for borrowing or grant repayment.

The revenue income stream provides the starting point for assessing the viability of new development: thorough capital and project risk appraisal is part of the decision-making over options. This may appear obvious, but many starting to make plans – families, voluntary organisations, professionals in the field of learning disability – may not be familiar with all the issues and need the advice and experience of others.

4.10 Elementary 'dos' and 'don'ts' for building development

Development for special needs can easily go wrong, through lack of experience, novel capital funding combinations, the difficulties of coping with additional regulations and the specific, complex needs of prospective residents. Below are some suggestions.

- Housing associations or registered social landlords (RSL) are now the main source of additional public sector rented provision. Private development is possible, either funded by individual family or groups, and can be arranged in a variety of ways.
- Make use of the social housing grant (SHG) from the Housing Corporation or local authority. Annual bid rounds result in allocation to RSLs, however local authorities SHG can come at any time and is not tied to the annual bid.
- Shared ownership is another attractive Housing Corporation funded programme for some circumstances, since it provides security of tenure (ownership) but takes only about half the SHG of the equivalent rented property. If a building is turned down as 'poor value for money', consider shared ownership. Shared ownership does not compromise entitlement to the *Supporting People* revenue grant. With shared ownership the individual can select their own property from the open market.
- New build is not the only route. 'Purchase and repair' or 'existing satisfactory properties (ESP), or 'acquisition and works', are all possibilities and are often quicker than new build. These are separate Housing Corporation programmes.
- A cost control system known as total cost indicators governs RSL costs; there are special allowances (multipliers) for housing for special needs, older people and for those with a disability, but approvals for special design or extra standards or amenities may still be difficult.
- The built form affects costs. Simpler forms are cheaper than complex structures. Bungalows are a more expensive form of accommodation and may appear to offer less 'value for money'.

- For ordinary dwellings 'design and build' procurement may be quicker and more economical than competitive tendering. However, it becomes even more important to specify precisely what is required at the outset.
- Architects vary in skills, interests, experience – visit similar completed buildings, take up references. Look at attention to detail in finished buildings. Ask for fee quotations. Have they designed for people with a learning disability before? Ensure that they will give the range of services required. Some architects are good at design, but not so good at on-site supervision of building – ensure that they can do what is needed. For cost estimates, quantity surveyors are the experts and it may be worth obtaining their advice.
- One approach to assessing a plan is to 'walk through' the building, room by room. Test the design against checklists of important features such as those in this book, e.g. the height of switches, handles, ease of access, whether part of the building will be noisy because of equipment (lifts, laundry, kitchen), how people will use the building, etc.
- Mobility standards do not have to be too expensive if incorporated at the outset. Lifetime Homes standards are a good compromise.

4.10.1 'Dos'

- Decide the composition of a project team and involve relevant organisations in the team – managers, service purchasers and user groups or advocates. Agree who fulfils the client function and instructs the architect. Never instruct the builder directly if you employ an architect or surveyor or other professional to manage the contracting.
- Fit building development within a broader plan (for an individual or organisation). Review against a set of criteria to be met: strategic fit, infrastructure and support requirements, care contract, building and design suited to special management or residents' needs, location and community presence, long and short term implications, fall back positions, legal advice or resource implications.
- Carry out thorough feasibility and risk appraisals: is there an 'exit' strategy or alternative use for the property, can it be resold without

substantial loss? Alternative use should always be taken into account, especially when buildings require private finance.

- Establish the strength of financial support for places provided, the interest of local authority or health purchasers or commissioners, and potential long-term demand.
- Make sure it is clear who the prospective tenants will be, and what their needs are now and will be in five years' time: will urgent local needs mysteriously evaporate or change? Anticipate forthcoming policy and legislative change and its impact over the medium term.
- Ensure as far as possible that the house, the project, the design, the location and the management arrangements will allow the defined need to be met. What are the possibilities if needs or the purpose of the project change? Is it possible to use the building differently, adapt or improve it, without enormous cost?
- Test capital costs assumptions (cost/person, cost/m^2), find comparables for value for money. What costs are eligible from different grant sources: housing, local authority and health? Identify potential abortive costs, excessive development and commissioning costs, and the impact of programme delays.
- Build white goods, insulation, fitted furniture and carpets into the contract if these are eligible for the social housing grant. Where there are ineligible costs or items funded by social services, health or charitable sources, make sure these can be separately identified.
- Create a clear specification for project development. Consult widely to get specification right. Look at similar services. Check if the very specialised requirements of some residents have been adequately catered for, and that furnishings, fittings and fixtures are suitable.
- Plan ahead: with new build, working with an RSL, it is likely to be three years from conception to completion.
- Hold pre-tender reviews to anticipate problems and suggest controls before tender stage, as well as post-tender/pre-contract reviews before contracts are signed.
- Pay attention to details, for example externally, to create a domestic feel, make the building attractive, in addition to secure. Internally, colour coding the doors, floor and walls, ensuring that bathroom and kitchen floors are non-slip, that all the furniture will fit, that there is

room for office space or storage, are all important details to bear in mind.

- Technology: consider what may be needed in the specification. Hard wired alarms may be more expensive and possibly not as useful now as dispersed alarms.
- Use feedback on design and tenant satisfaction surveys to inform future development.

4.10.2 'Don'ts'

- Innovation or tight deadlines increase the risk of mistakes, resulting in cost over runs, or design errors being discovered after handover. Don't forget the possible cost of programme delays within the first year; there are so many possible causes: legal, funding or statutory approvals, inclement weather, etc.
- Specification is frequently the weak link; if it is not right, you will either not get what is wanted or incur expensive changes.
- Don't be led too eagerly by opportunity, as such development brings risks – don't skip the assessment of viability and objective appraisal.
- Don't overlook restrictive covenants – obtain good advice or insurance.
- Don't discover planning, fire, environmental health, registered care or any other crucial requirements too late in the day. Accommodating the variety of requirements specified by statutory authorities, commissioners and clients while still aiming for non-institutional results is not easy.
- Don't forget the funders' requirements for probity and accountability.
- Don't ignore the revenue budget just because the capital development appears value for money – do they *both* add up?
- It is very easy to generate costs which have not been allowed for in the capital budget. Poor initial information about needs, unsuitable design leading to changes, contract variations during project development, unforeseen or additional requirements can all push budgets over the limits of affordability or grant funds.
- Planning objections can halt or delay a project; neighbours can take action for noise and nuisance under environmental health law. For

potential or actual tenants there is the risk of local hostility and harassment. Don't underestimate the real difficulties but don't be overawed either. Be reasonable – neighbours may be nervous.
- Don't overlook costs in use, for example: ease of maintenance, accessibility for maintenance and potential maintenance costs, estimated life of materials, durability of equipment and service requirements.

4.11 Neighbours

There is a normal anxiety about new neighbours and this is exaggerated when they do not appear to be an ordinary family household. Additionally, there are the more-than-normal worries and complaints which have to be assessed and addressed, however irrational they may at first seem.

There are issues about managing the proper introduction of a new home into a street or community: issues of noise, privacy, parking and intensity of use and about the suitability of the location for the proposed household.

There are legal, planning and statutory control matters to be dealt with and other requirements that the local authorities, social services, housing or planning departments may require of a developer or manager of a new service.

The starting-point should be a realistic appraisal of the project and its introduction into the community – a community audit which would assess the strengths and weaknesses of the project and its location:

- concentrations of special housing should be avoided;
- a realistic appraisal should be made of likely local fears or concerns including possible causes of local nuisance, intensity of use, staff numbers, parking, noise, or any items which may cause reasonable concern for neighbours;

- any conflicting requirements of developer, manager, funders and local authority departments need to be identified, e.g. as to size, design and layout.

The initial appraisal needs to take account of what will count as successful community presence, how to minimise real risks or concerns, and the possible strength of local objections which might prevent the project from going ahead. In the case of the likelihood that the scheme can be prevented then the developer must have a strategy for reasonably countering such objections.

After an appraisal of the project a strategy should be agreed between those concerned with the development, the managers, developers, consultants and local authorities.

It is not possible to avoid problems entirely by good planning and forethought but risks can be reduced. It is often possible to see where these risks have been missed or underestimated because of a lack of attention to matters we have suggested for a community audit. With the general support of the local authority, which is in any case a prerequisite for access to public funding, it is difficult for unreasonable objections to be sustained and as a price for that support the developer or manager for a housing project must be prepared to accommodate the wishes of the local authority. But beyond this, unless there are any other enforceable objections to development, the key to the project's success must be the achievement of satisfactory 'community presence' which should benefit both the newcomers and the existing neighbourhood. The way in which a manager and residents wish to achieve this as they introduce themselves to their new neighbourhood should be, as far as is practically possible, for them to decide.

When a house is open, anxiety usually dissipates as relationships with neighbours build. A protracted dispute may sometimes persist but it is very rare that good management cannot produce improvement.

5. Standards

5.1 Earlier published guidance

Only two special guides have appeared on this issue, the first of which is 25 years old. The first is on design[1] and the second on standards generally for homes.[2]

The 1973 design guide was firmly based on a residential care model but recognised that people could benefit not only from this but from more independence in group homes, foster homes or lodgings and even considered the use of council properties.

The guidance emphasised the importance of location and access to community facilities, shops and amenities and integration in neighbourhoods. There was an idea of learning independence within the 'hostel' as a stage to moving on and this led to a theory of size which should be large enough to allow for choice in relationships but small enough for local community integration. A range of 16 to 25 people was suggested, very different from the advice from the 2001 White Paper or Care Standards guidance.

The needs of individuals and particular disabilities were acknowledged to be important, as well as the views of clients, and day-time and evening activities. The outstanding element of the guidance, which is very detailed and prescriptive, is that the total space per person should be between 39 and 46 m^2 – a standard which has probably rarely been achieved.

[1] Department of Health and Security, *Local Authority Building Note No 8: Residential Accommodation for Mentally Handicapped Adults* (1973).
[2] Department of Health/SSI, *Guidance on Standards for Residential Care Needs for People with Learning Difficulties,* London (1992).

The second *Guidance on Standards* says nothing specific on size or minimum space standards and remains based on residential care models, but it recognises that:

- The focus on 'an ordinary life' has meant that attention has primarily been paid to making available the same scale and type of housing used by the general population.
- '... the design or conversion of a residential home ... demands a compromise between domestic and institutional architecture that accommodates the needs of both residents and staff.'
- Over the last 20 years increasing attention has been paid to the impact that the built environment and physical surroundings have on the quality of life experienced by users. The benefits of individual privacy are now accepted and an increasing proportion of people with learning disabilities have a single bedroom.
- The importance of good quality, comfortable and well designed furnishings and decor is acknowledged. Inspectors should expect that agencies and managers will pay attention to the environment in which people are living and that needs of users are given primacy over those of the staff.

This guidance is largely overtaken by the new minimum standards required for registered care homes which are dealt with below.

There are additional design considerations when, besides a learning difficulty, people have physical or sensory disabilities, may be autistic or have other complex needs. Some residents may inflict more damage on a building or fittings than usual wear and tear. People may need more space than usual. If they have poor motor skills they may be more vulnerable to injury. Those who are autistic may be unusually sensitive to their environments in sometimes unexpected ways. Accommodation may need to be more robust and designed to allow for more demanding use. Budgets should allow for high levels of wear and tear and renewal of fittings.

In the following sections there are some further comments on physical and sensory disability, and complex needs.

5.2 Standards for registered social landlords

The Housing Corporation provides design guidance for registered social landlords in *Scheme Development Standards*.[3] This document is predominantly guidance for affordable general needs housing but includes important requirements relating to accessibility, energy ratings, size of properties, and additional requirements such as 'Lifetime Homes'.

Scheme Development Standards cover general needs housing but also refer to other types of accommodation where different standards are required. These are listed below. Category 1 and 2 sheltered housing is included because these provide relevant standards for small self-contained units. The National Housing Federation also provides useful guidance.[4]

Table 5.1 Scheme Development Standards

Housing for the elderly	**Category 1:** self-contained accommodation with an element of warden support and additional communal facilities. **Category 2:** self-contained accommodation for less active elderly with a warden or 24-hour peripatetic support and additional communal facilities. Frail elderly and extra care supported accommodation, which may be either shared or self-contained, for frail older persons. Includes warden or 24-hour emergency care, the full range of communal facilities, plus additional special features, including wheelchair user environments and supportive management.

[3] Housing Corporation, *Scheme Development Standards* (2000).
[4] National Housing Federation, *Standards and Quality in Development*, London (1998).

Table 5.1 Scheme Development Standards – *continued*

Shared housing	Accommodation predominantly for single persons, which includes a degree of sharing between tenants of some facilities (e.g. kitchens, bathrooms, living room) and may include an element of support and or additional communal facilities.
Supported housing	Accommodation, which may be either shared or self-contained, designed to meet the special needs of particular user groups (see the Housing Corporation's *Guide to Supported Housing*) and which includes supportive management and may also include additional communal facilities.
Housing for wheelchair users	Accommodation, which may be either shared or self-contained, designed for independent living by physically disabled people and wheelchair users. Where such accommodation is incorporated within schemes containing communal facilities, an appropriate proportion of all such facilities should be wheelchair accessible.
Communal facilities	Ancillary communal accommodation, the range of which comprises: common rooms to accommodate tenants and occasional visitors, chair storage and kitchenette for tea-making, warden's office, call systems, laundry and guest rooms.

5.3 Registration as a care home or as domiciliary services

Government policy for community care aims to promote independence, while protecting service users' safety. The new regulatory framework under the Care Standards Act 2000 aims to ensure high standards of care and to protect vulnerable people. The guidance strongly recommends seeking advice from the National Care Standards Commission from April 2002.

Accommodation may not need to be registered under the Care Standards Act 2000, but the minimum standards recommended may usefully influence design and allow for the option of registration. The Care Homes Regulations 2001 No. 3965 provide for the proper provision of welfare, care and supervision, including arrangements for staffing, furnishing, equipment, facilities, repair, fire precautions, risk of accidents, environmental health, record-keeping, recreation and occupation.

The guidelines (*see* Appendix 4) deal with the size of bedrooms, staffing levels and the need for sleep-in staff, the layout, requirement for a separate utility room, together with features such as door closers, signs, fire alarms and extinguishers, some of which can be obtrusive. The aim to provide an ordinary home may be difficult to achieve consistent with fire, environmental health, building regulation and registered home requirements.

The Care Standards Act 2000 specifies which establishments must be registered as care homes from April 2002. These are establishments that provide accommodation together with nursing or personal care for people who are or have been ill, who have or have had a mental disorder, who are disabled or infirm, or who are or have been dependent on alcohol or drugs.

Grant conditions under *Supporting People*[5] are currently being determined. These will not allow for funding of registered care homes from *Supporting People* funds, other than transitionally for care homes previously funded (in part) by social housing management grant.

5.3.1 What is a care home?

The definition of a care home in the Care Standards Act 2000 differs slightly from the definition in the Registered Homes Act 1984 in that it does not refer to the provision of board. It is an 'establishment which provides accommodation together with nursing or personal care'.

So whether the accommodation is provided by an establishment together with personal or nursing care has to be determined. It may be relevant that these elements are provided by separate individuals or companies.

Where a person rents a flat and receives domiciliary care, there is no connection between the landlord and the care agency. Where it appears that both come together as a package from an 'establishment' it appears to be registerable as a care home.

In many supported housing schemes, personal care is being provided to people in their own homes, whether they are an owner-occupier or a tenant, and it does not matter that some of the accommodation is shared.

5.3.2 What is personal care?

Draft guidance from the Department of Health[6] says that the requirement under the Care Standards Act 2000 for registration as a care home is only triggered where personal care is provided which is:

- assistance with bodily functions such as feeding, bathing, and toileting.

[5] Department of Transport, Local Government and the Regions, *Supporting People, Administrative Guidance* (2001).
[6] Department of Health, *Residential Care, Housing Care and Support and 'Supporting People'* (2001).

Registration as a domiciliary care agency would also be required if such assistance is provided or:

- care which falls just short of assistance with bodily functions, but still involving physical and intimate touching, including activities such as helping a person get out of a bath and helping them to get dressed.

Non-physical care, emotional and psychological support do not of themselves trigger a requirement for registration with the National Care Standards Commission.

5.3.3 Domiciliary care

Where an agency arranges to provide personal care to a person in their own home, it must register as a domiciliary care agency. A domiciliary care agency is defined as 'an undertaking which consists of or includes arranging the provision of personal care in their own homes for persons who by reason of illness, infirmity or disability are unable to provide it for themselves without assistance'. Personal care delivered to people in their own homes will be regulated under the provisions in the Act covering domiciliary care agencies. This will ensure that vulnerable people receiving personal care in their own homes get the protection they need.

5.3.4 Adult placements

Adult placement provides accommodation and support normally to one or two adults, placed through an Adult Placement Scheme in the family home of an Adult Placement Carer. In cases where personal care is provided, carers are registered in respect of their own home and must take into account the National Minimum Standards when making decisions about registration.

5.3.5 Standards for shared housing and residential care for younger adults

The National Minimum Standards for Care Homes for Younger Adults are the core requirements for care homes for adults aged 18 to 65 years.

Although this guide is mainly concerned with physical design matters they are based on the following key values:

- autonomy: promotion of individual autonomy, self-determination and choice, and control over decision-making;
- attainment: recognition of individual ability and potential for personal development, and of the social and environmental barriers to achieving potential;
- citizenship: maintenance of entitlements associated with citizenship under UK law and the Human Rights Act 1998, including protection from discrimination, harassment, exploitation or abuse, neglect, degrading or inhuman treatment;
- individuality: respect for individuality, privacy and dignity and maintenance of self-esteem in all situations;
- diversity: respect for age, ethnic and cultural diversity, and promotion of equal opportunity;
- well-being: promotion of physical, emotional and spiritual well-being;
- inclusion: promotion of social and economic inclusion and participation in community life.

5.3.6 Physical standards

Further detail is given in Appendix 4 but the key points on physical standards are given in draft Department of Health minimum standards guidance[7] including:

- minimum total average living space (bedroom and communal space) of 14.1 m^2 (17.1 m^2 for wheelchair users);
- new homes: maximum of 20 people with no more than 10 sharing a staff group, a dining area and other common facilities; existing, larger homes on this basis by 2007;
- the home offers access to local amenities, local transport and relevant support services as appropriate;
- the premises are fully accessible to all service users; homes accommodating wheelchair users provide level access and 800 mm doorways throughout;

[7] Department of Health, *Care Homes for Younger Adults: National Minimum Standards* (2001).

- the premises meet the requirements of the local fire service and environmental health department, health and safety and building Acts and Regulations, and from 2004 the Disability Discrimination Act 1995 Part 3;
- shared rooms are phased out by 2004 unless people want to share;
- single rooms in current use have at least 10 m^2 usable floor space and wash hand basin (unless there is an en-suite);
- single rooms in current use accommodating wheelchair users have at least 12 m^2;
- WCs are shared by no more than two people, and bathrooms by three. These facilities are to be near service users' bedrooms;
- first time new build registrations provide individual en-suite bedrooms with at least 12 m^2 usable floor space;
- domestic scale kitchen and laundry;
- a private area for visitors, consultations or treatment;
- a separate smoking area if the home does not have a 'no smoking' policy;
- laundry facilities are sited so that soiled articles, clothing and infected linen are not carried through kitchens.

5.4 Physical disability

Physical disability, cerebral palsy or other impairments of movement occur in 20 to 30 per cent of people with severe learning disability. The starting point for thinking about design includes the following key points:

- if a building is designed to be usable by someone in a wheelchair it will probably be appropriate for all disabilities;
- people with learning disabilities can now expect a life span which compares with the general population, so it makes sense to construct buildings that can be adapted easily and economically. An influential example of long term thinking about flexible use is Lifetime Homes;[8]

[8] J. Brewerton and D, Darton, *Designing Lifetime Homes*, York Publishing (1996).

- Lifetime Homes are 'ordinary housing' not 'special needs' accommodation, designed so that people with moderate mobility needs can be accommodated in general needs housing;
- quality of life can often be improved by careful consideration of the individual's (and carer's) specific needs and wishes.

The standards for care homes[9] recommend adaptations and equipment to maximise independence in homes offering a service to people with physical disabilities and recommends specialist equipment should be provided as needed for the individual, including:

- moving equipment/overhead tracking for hoists;
- stair rails, lifts;
- environmental control system;
- appropriate bathroom fittings/equipment;
- call alarm systems;
- lowered light switches, work surfaces, window openings;
- storage/recharging facilities for wheelchairs/mobility equipment.

The need for aids, adaptations and equipment should be assessed and recommended by an occupational therapist or other specialist.

Detailed design guidance has been provided by RIBA[10] and RADAR,[11] by the National Wheelchair Housing Association Group[12] and the Centre for Accessible Environments.[13]

5.4.1 Wheelchair-friendly building

When the client is a registered social landlord (RSL) what they can spend on a building is controlled by a system of total cost indicators (TCI) published and supervised by the Housing Corporation. The Corporation

[9] Department of Health, 2001, n 7 above.

[10] RIBA and Chartered Institute of Housing, *Housing for Disabled People* (1998).

[11] Royal Association for Disability and Rehabilitation, *The Disability Discrimination Act 1995: A Guide to Goods and Services Provision*, London (1999).

[12] National Wheelchair Housing Design Group, *Wheelchair Housing Design Guide* (1997).

[13] Centre for Accessible Environments, *Designing for Accessibility* (1993).

also requires RSLs to conform to a set of Scheme Development Standards. These in turn require RSLs to meet the specifications set out in the *Wheelchair Housing Design Guide.*[14] If the RSL can certify it has met this standard it can get more money through a higher 'multiplier' which has the effect of increasing the TCI limit.

Architects are recommended to consult the same document for detailed guidance on designing for wheelchair users. An extract from the Scheme Development Standards covering wheelchair design requirements is given in Appendix 5.

The essence of designing for wheelchair users is to make getting around easy and equipment and fittings like window furniture accessible and easy to use:

- reasonable space to get around, turn a wheelchair and access equipment and storage;
- flat floors and no barriers;
- bathroom and kitchens on the same level as living areas and detailed attention to easy use of these two areas in particular;
- wide doors;
- drive-in showers rather than baths;
- worktops to get wheelchairs under;
- suitable electrical fittings at a different height to normal;
- fittings that are easy to operate without great strength.

5.4.2 Smart Homes

The Joseph Rowntree Foundation is responsible for several Smart Homes[15] demonstration projects including fitting out a new bungalow in Hartrigg Oaks, their retirement village, and retro-fitting an Edwardian house. Smart Homes are largely about making it easier for people with physical or sensory limitations to live a normal life, in ostensibly ordinary housing, although some of the technology tested might be of general appeal.

[14] National Wheelchair Housing Design Group, 1997, n 12 above.
[15] T. Venables and C. Taylor, *Smart Homes: A Specification Guide,* York Publishing (2001).

Defining features of the Smart Home demonstrations have been:

- controls can be operated in a variety of ways including manually, by remote infra-red controls, a touch-screen, over the telephone or programmed to operate automatically;
- devices are linked together to form an integrated system.

The specific devices demonstrated and their possibilities include:

- **lighting and heating controls:** entering a room automatically turns the light on, pressing the door bell flashes the light on and off (useful for hard of hearing), getting out of bed at night turns on a light and a path to the toilet is illuminated, thermometers, heat detectors and smoke alarms are combined in a single fitting – as with all devices, they can be programmed or combined in a variety of ways and linked to a call centre;
- **doors:** open automatically by small motors when approached or switched on;
- **taps:** can be controlled in a variety of ways including hot and cold buttons or sinks that can be filled by remote control;
- **door entry:** a picture of a caller is displayed on the TV (which is switched on if not already on);
- **central locking:** a fob placed against an alarm panel locks all doors and windows;
- **windows:** can be opened and closed electronically;
- **kitchen unit and sink heights** can be adjusted;
- **curtains or blinds:** can be opened and closed, again driven by small motors, and programmed to open and close at the onset of daylight or darkness;
- **safety:** a variety of monitoring devices based on infra-red and other sensors will detect gas leaks (and shut off gas), intruders, fire, smoke etc.

The Joseph Rowntree Foundation demonstrated one example of how devices can be linked and programmed together:

> A button on the hand-held remote control labelled 'Good morning' is pressed, which automatically turns on the kettle, opens the curtains

and windows, and turns on the radio and the shower … The 'Good night' button switches off the lights as well as locking the windows and setting the alarms, and turns designated equipment off.

5.4.3 Lifetime Homes

Developed and tested by the Joseph Rowntree Foundation, Lifetime Homes[16] have become adopted as the basic standard for general needs housing by a number of local authorities and Housing Associations.

The Lifetime Homes standard consists of 16 design or construction requirements illustrated in Figure 5.1. The intention is to create housing that is inherently easier to live in by someone with mobility problems but can also be more easily and cheaply adapted as needs change. The design features have been chosen with care so that the property should in fact be more attractive to everyone – disabled or not – without features that obviously identify it as for a disabled person. The name derives from the idea that the design features make the house inherently easier to use at each stage in the life cycle, from housing young children to becoming less mobile in later life, and also that the property can be adapted to meet mobility difficulties.

A Lifetime Home requires the 16 relevant standards listed in Figure 5.1 to be incorporated. These standards have been divided into three sections: Access, Inside the Home and Fixtures and Fittings. In addition, all Lifetime Homes are designed to be capable of modification if a member of the household is unable to climb stairs.

(i) Access

1. Car parking space potentially 3.3 m wide.
2. Distance from car space to home should be kept to a minimum.
3. Approach to entrance should be level or gently sloping.
4. Entrances should be level, with shelter and an outside light.
5. Lifts need to be wheelchair accessible, with controls at low level.

[16] Brewerton and Darton, 1996, n 8 above.

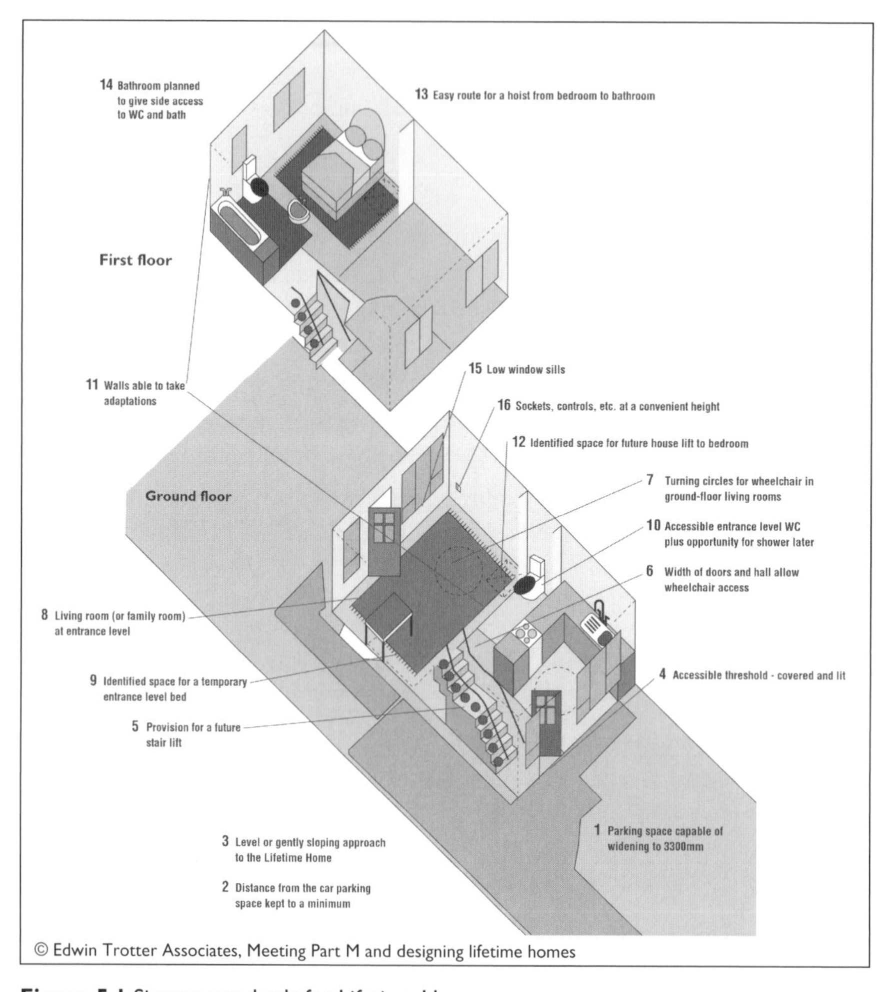

© Edwin Trotter Associates, Meeting Part M and designing lifetime homes

Figure 5.1 Sixteen standards for Lifetime Homes

(ii) Inside the home

6. Entrance doors need a clear opening of 800 mm and 750 mm for internal doors.
7. A 1,500 mm turning circle for wheelchairs in main rooms, kitchen and hallway.
8. Sitting room at entrance level.
9. Two storey houses should have a bed space on the ground floor.
10. A wheelchair accessible WC downstairs with potential for a shower space.

11. Bathroom/WC walls strong enough for fixing grab-rails.
12. Provision for installing stairlift or through-the-floor lift.
13. Bath/bedroom ceiling strong enough for a hoist and provision for future door opening.
14. Bathroom designed for ease of access.

(iii) Fixtures and fittings

15. Easy to open windows with sills no higher than 800 mm.
16. All switches and controls to be positioned between 600–1,200 mm from floor level.

Features which may generally appeal include downstairs cloakroom, porch at front door, car parking near to house. Features that allow for modification include some construction materials and details in the bathroom to allow future fixing of rails and adaptation in the construction of the floor in case a through-the-floor lift is required at some point. There are a few matters of practical detail to bear in mind, and draw the builder's attention to, because they differ from normal building practice. For example raising sockets well above the height of the skirting board, level thresholds throughout the dwelling including at the front door and different detailing to stop rainwater ingress. David Bonnet,[17] an architect who uses a wheelchair, has made a number of suggestions:

- **Clear opening of internal doors:** should be 750 mm and front doors 800 mm. This requires doors wider than these dimensions to allow for door steps and the thickness of the door itself.
- **Window handles and levers:** need to be within the 600–1,200 mm 'reach zone' of a wheelchair user. Turn lock casement windows are, e.g. out of reach. Better are espagnolite bolts operated by one hand or top hung casements.
- **Window sills:** should be no higher than 800 mm to provide a view out from a seated position or when in bed.
- **Bathroom:** wall-hung hand basin rather than pedestal mounted provides more clear floor space under the basin. Wall construction

[17] D. Bonnett and N. King, *Shared Ownership: Lifetime Homes, Making it Work,* Shared Ownership Lifetime Homes Group (1997).

should allow for the fixing of grab rails, and drive-in showers are more useable than a bath.

- **Switches and controls:** should again be within the 600–1,200 mm reach zone. This includes stop cocks, electrical circuit breakers, light switches, electrical power sockets. (However, for some people with learning disabilities, some of these controls may need to be within cabinets or secure boxes. Other controls need to be selected for simplicity and clarity of operation, e.g. colour coded.)
- **Kitchens:** there needs to be space to turn a wheelchair and open cupboard doors and drawers, about 1,200–1,500 mm. Some worktops that allow a wheelchair to go under the work surface, normally close to the sink. Ideally, adjustable worktop heights for different 'zones' of the kitchen.
- **Lifting and handling:** some people with learning disabilities are very severely physically disabled as well and require staff to assist them, e.g. in and out of bed, onto a toilet. A ceiling mounted track and hoist system in some (or all rooms) can be installed to considerably aid the process and give the individual some greater privacy and dignity. Health and safety legislation designed to protect staff has had a considerable impact on employers, making consideration of the installation of tracks for some individuals a suitable option.

5.5 Assistive technology

At its broadest, assistive technology could cover everything from passive fittings such as a grab rail to assist a physically disabled person do something more easily through to a very sophisticated, computer-controlled array of devices that actively do things directly for a person, such as helping them to talk (as for example Professor Stephen Hawking, the well-known scientist who has Motor Neurone Disease).

In this section we focus on electronic equipment that can in various ways make life easier or safer for someone with a learning disability.

5.5.1 The assistive technology context

Knowing the origins and possibilities should help the designer or commissioner to make the best use of assistive technology.

There has been relatively little attention paid to assistive technology specifically in relation to people with a learning disability and their housing and support. The Joseph Rowntree Foundation, who have pioneered and funded much research in relation to physical disability and older people such as their Smart Homes, advise that they have not undertaken any work in relation to learning disability. In consequence, many of the devices and technological solutions are 'borrowed' from their application to older people.

Much (but not all) of the technology can be relatively easily and cheaply purpose-built by assembling standard components. There are a number of companies able to do this. Where it is believed that a problem might be solved by a piece of technology, the fact that the right 'product' on the market cannot immediately be found does not mean it cannot be created. In the context of the relatively high annual support costs of some individuals, even the one-off development and construction cost of a unique device might make economic sense.

A number of devices are capable of being used flexibly and adapted for a different role to that for which they are marketed. As an example, units that are primarily designed to function as an alarm system for older people who have a fall, sending a signal to a 'call centre' that monitors calls 24-hours a day, can equally well direct calls to a carer living nearby in a core and cluster scheme or the project key worker in a 'community network' like *Keyring* (a service provider supporting a group of individual tenants in a neighbourhood).

Not all devices that are to do a particular job actually achieve what they claim. They may work in different ways which affects the outcome. The message is to seek independent evidence of manufacturer's claims and think through the implications of how the device works. As an example there are more than a dozen different devices on the market designed to detect hypothermia, a cause of a large number of deaths amongst older people. The devices work in different ways. One group is worn by the person and monitors body temperature (and possibly other functions), a second group monitors the environment, triggering an alarm if criteria are met, e.g. below a set temperature for more than a certain length of time.

Independent tests concluded that of the devices evaluated those worn on the person would trigger an alarm once hypothermia had set in and often after the point when an older person would be capable of taking action to reverse the condition. The devices monitoring the environment could alert the individual or call centre of the approach of hypothermia before this danger point. To give another example, a fall detector attached to a belt can be triggered if the wearer simply drops their trousers when going to the toilet.

Finally, in relation to people with learning disabilities there are different categories of assistive technology:

- **Communications:** various high and low technology equipment is available to aid communication. Low technology examples are pictures of food illustrating a menu or pictures of people showing who is in the duty rota. High technology examples include the software programme 'Widgit' which turns typed text into pictorial symbols and pictures, or hand-held computers that show illustrations on a touch screen which can be used to make choices and express preferences. One system displays icons on a screen and when touched they speak a message. The system can be linked and programmed for the individual's requirements and is called 'Icon Speak'.
- **Monitoring and control:** these are systems which monitor either the person or environment, informing carers or a remote 'call centre' of potential dangers or changes. Most commonplace are fire, gas, smoke, intruder and similar alarms. In sheltered schemes, alarm systems in each property linked to a warden and/or a call centre have been a defining feature. In a block of flats, a door entry system with two-way speech should be specified. Many devices can both monitor and control automatically the thermostat on the central heating or a thermostat and control on a shower or bath.

- **Supporting activity:** the third group use technology to make it easier or possible for a disabled person to carry out some tasks themselves. This is illustrated in the Smart Homes' use of motors to open and close down windows and curtains, stair lifts and track and hoist systems (see case study 6.1).

Assistive technology focused on communication can be very helpful but is mostly not necessary to specify at the design stage other than to ensure an adequate (abundance) of electrical sockets and telephone points throughout the building.

Technology that supports activity may well need to be specified at design stage but is most likely to relate to a physical or sensory impairment rather than learning disability. The key thing to pay attention to is how the technology will be controlled by the user. Simpler controls or fully programmed ones are likely to be essential. Many devices can be programmed (or over-ridden) remotely using the telephone system or other technology.

At the heart of user control is the type of switching specified. The possibilities include:

- air pressure;
- pressure mats – stepping on a mat activates a switch, e.g. getting out of bed or stepping on a front door mat can be detected;
- dome switches – these can be large, coloured, etc. (see case study 6.1);
- bend and click;
- foot switch;
- sound;
- hand print;
- pull;
- breaking infra-red beam.[18]

[18] These and many other switches can be seen or obtained from Assistive Education and Therapy Technologies, Unit 13, Business and Innovation Centre, Angel Way, Lester Hills, Bradford, West Yorks, BD7 1BX, telephone 01274 841342.

5.5.2 Monitoring and control: in general

It is in this third area that there are the widest range of devices immediately applicable to people with learning disabilities, information that is useful to consider at the design stage. This section begins with an explanation of the use of alarms among older people.

Alarm systems were a defining feature of sheltered housing for older people. Originally the system and wiring were built into the building and referred to as 'hard wired'. Each dwelling (and communal areas) had several pull cords used in an emergency to alert on-site wardens to a fall, illness or other mishap. Wardens from their offices, flats or from around the scheme could speak directly to the resident via an intercom system also installed in each resident dwelling. They could then deal with the situation themselves, call relatives or other emergency services.

Over the last 30 years there have been some changes. In order to cover times when the wardens, now often called scheme managers, were not available and meet the needs of the growing number of schemes with no warden, service alarm systems are linked to 'call centres' via the telephone network. Each centre processes alarm calls through a computer system which identifies the caller, displays their personal details such as known illness and medication, and the operators can, just like the warden, talk directly to the caller who has triggered the alarm and take the best action. They keep lists of key holders and relatives/neighbours. Being linked to an alarm monitoring system can cost less than £1 per week and it is a highly competitive market.

A variety of devices have been developed, including brooches, wrist bands and pendants, which trigger an alarm from a distance to cover the eventuality of falling some way from a pull cord or even outside. They typically operate up to 30–100 m from the dwelling.

The call centres have developed the ability to monitor, and sometimes control, an array of detectors rather than just respond to a direct call from a resident. So, e.g., cameras outside the scheme or at the front door can be monitored. The front door can be opened to let callers in or allow the emergency services to gain access. The technology has developed so that it is no longer necessary to have expensive 'hard wired' systems. It is now very easy to link anyone with a telephone socket to a call centre, which can be anywhere in the country or next door, via what is termed a 'dispersed alarm'. So just about everybody with a learning disability wherever they live in the community can access call centre services. The system can also be programmed to call local staff, including on a mobile phone (although this is not always reliable) before contacting the call centre. Some of the call centres have enhanced their own services by employing mobile staff (or linking with another organisation that does this). This means that they can dispatch their own staff to respond to an emergency call.

Finally, a few care providers working with older people have recognised that the emergency alarm system is in practice widely used for things other than an emergency and actively encourage residents to use the system for routine communication.

5.5.3 Dispersed alarms

It is this equipment that has replaced the previous 'hard wired' alarm technology. In essence a dispersed alarm is a box that sits alongside the phone. At the simplest, pressing a button on the box or a radio trigger contained in say a pendant or wrist-strap activates the unit to dial into a monitoring centre or ring a pre-determined number which could be a care provider or staff member on call. Whoever receives the call can talk to the person through the unit and also hear them. In effect it acts like a hands-free phone.

There are a wide range of dispersed units with different facilities, but most are capable of doing considerably more than this. They are likely to be able to:

- monitor an array of passive infra-red and other devices sending messages to the monitoring centre or care provider, e.g. if someone leaves or enters the house after a certain time;

- prompt the resident to do certain things via a pre-recorded message, e.g. 'Today is Thursday and you go to college';
- monitor the taking of medication via a pill dispenser and prompt the user to take the medicine, ultimately going on to alert the monitoring centre/care provider if medication has been missed;
- sound an alarm and/or alert the call centre or individual via a pre-recorded message, if certain things happen or are not done, e.g. the front door is left open for more than a certain period or the hob on the cooker is left on or if there is no movement in a dwelling;
- alert the call centre and the carers if the person goes beyond a pre-defined distance from the home, e.g. past the corner shop, via a proximity alarm.

5.5.4 Monitoring and control devices

We have given examples of some devices explaining the progress of 'telealarm' technology and the development of dispersed alarms and control centres.

There are opportunities to support people with learning disabilities, in ordinary housing or in specialist provision, through a combination of traditional visiting or on-site support (domiciliary care) and new and old assistive devices and communication technologies. The role of assistive technology in relation to people with learning disabilities is to:

- assist them by providing a 'barrier free' environment that enables and is usable and controllable by the individual;
- create a safer environment.

This is achieved by a combination of community alarms, telecare/remote health care monitoring, support and assistive technology. As explained above with respect to the Smart Home demonstration, devices can be linked to form an integrated system controlled in different ways either by the user or carer or remotely.

Monitoring and control devices depend on some form of sensor connected to an internal and external communication system – these may be hard wired, wireless or function via a telephone network (either a land line or cell phone). They can be linked to programmable controls. At its simplest this might be an instruction 'If room temperature goes below 15°C then turn up heat until 20°C'.

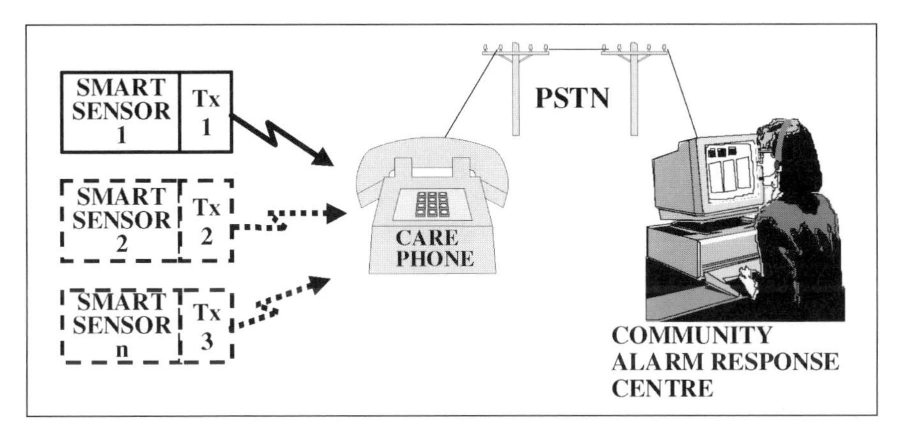

Figure 5.2 First generation telecare system

Figure 5.2 shows a block diagram of a telecare system built on the basic community alarm system. The key elements are a number of discrete 'smart' sensors which communicate wirelessly with a Care Phone. The Care Phone must interpret the alarm messages and convey their exact meaning unambiguously to the human operator at the control or response centre.

Devices available in addition to those already mentioned (smoke, heat, intruder alarm, gas detector, proximity sensor, pressure mats etc.), include:

- **Fred:** fall detector – this can be worn on a belt or wrist;
- **Brenda:** monitors bed usage – picks up unexpected absence;
- **Bert:** monitors and prompts taking of medication;
- **Flora:** flood alarm which detects excessive water on floor;
- **Hettie:** warns of very low or high temperature;
- **Esme:** provides warning of wet sheets or incontinence pad.

These devices are referred to as first generation telecare. Second generation developments provide for a much more comprehensive 'life style' monitoring, greater use of computers and different types of sensors (activity, event, environmental, utility, physiological). They are linked together and connect in a more 'intelligent' fashion. So, e.g. the intruder alarm does not need to be switched on and off because it knows from other sensors what the occupancy of the home is. At present the monitoring devices, beyond the basic dispersed alarm unit, most commonly used for people with learning disabilities are:[19]

- fall detectors, because of the incidence of epilepsy;
- sensors which alert staff when someone leaves the building, or a defined environment, because of the possibility of someone wandering (or running away);
- special beds for people with epilepsy.

5.6 Sensory impairment

Sensory impairment is far more common in people with learning disabilities than in the general population: 48 per cent of those with a learning disability have at least a moderate single impairment.[20] Hearing loss and visual impairment have each been estimated at about 40 per cent of people with severe learning disability. Hearing and visual problems are particularly common among people with Down's Syndrome.

In both cases attention to design details, equipment and technology can all play a part in assisting in daily life. Homes offering a service to people with a sensory impairment provide specialist aids and adaptations:

- hearing loops, microphones, minicom, textphones or videophone;
- additional and/or anti-glare lighting, colour contrasting, tactile symbols, varied textural surfaces;

[19] This section on assistive technology draws on work by Dr K. Doughty and his associates at Technology in Healthcare, telephone 01248 718020; email: research@tech-healthcare.demon.co.uk
[20] OPCS, *The Prevalence of Disability in Great Britain,* London, HMSO (1989).

- fluorescent or padded hazards/obstructions (where they cannot be removed);
- computer for user's personal use;
- TV with video recorder and subtitling facility/sign language.

Provision of aids, adaptations and equipment follows assessment by, and meets the recommendations of, an occupational therapist or other suitably qualified specialist.

Safety systems and equipment are appropriate for people with mobility/sensory problems, e.g. flashing light fire alarms, magnetic fire doors. Further guidance on these adaptations to buildings can be sought from the Royal National Institute for the Blind (RNIB)[21] and SENSE.[22]

5.6.1 Visual impairment

Nearly 90 per cent of people registered blind have some residual vision. In design terms it helps to know the form their ability to use residual vision takes:

- long or short sighted;
- tunnel or peripheral vision;
- night blind;
- sensitive to light.

Optometrists can carry out tests for these in ways which do not require any ability to read. The main guiding principles to consider, to help people use the building and equipment, are:

- **Contrasts in colour:** ensuring that the floor contrasts with walls; sockets and door handles contrast with walls; that there is colour contrast between surfaces and surface edges.

[21] RNIB and SIGN, *Visibly Better, RNIB Accreditation for Residential and Nursing Homes,* London, RNIB (1999).
[22] SENSE, the National Deafblind and Rubella Association, *Standards for Services for People who are Deafblind or have Dual Sensory Impairment,* London, SSI (2000).

- **Use of touch and sound in addition to residual vision:** contrasting textures can be used to define walls or floors. Floor coverings can be varied, producing different sounds, to help define separate areas.
- **Providing cues:** through the physical design and layout of the building, as well as designing out obvious dangers, e.g. rounded edges to where walls meet, built in furniture and ample sockets for electrical equipment to avoid trailing flexes.
- **Use assistive technology:** to counter impairment or warn of danger.

A process for those designing or briefing recommended by the RNIB is shown in Table 5.2.

Table 5.2 RNIB recommended design process checklist

Stage	Look at:
Review each room	Colour contrast, lighting and non-visual clues to find your way around
Function of room	A room used often in a similar way might have a 'route' defined by colour, sound, texture, e.g. path from bedroom to bathroom. In a group home each person's own room door might be given a personal colour
Overall themes of building	Consistent use of colour and materials. Do all toilets have the same colour door? Do kitchens all have tiled floors?
Consistency	Light switches similar and at same height, handrails consistent in style and shape
What needs to be variable	Lighting controllable – dimmer switches
Safety outside	Lighting at night, steps and paths illuminated and contrast with surrounding area

5.6.2 Designing for visual impairment: a checklist

Ideas for different parts of the building are laid out as a checklist overleaf which build on the principles of using colour, contrast, texture, light and sound.

Checklist for visual impairment design

(i) Front entrance

- [ ] Front door contrasts with surrounding area
- [ ] Raised numerals at eye level
- [ ] Door handles contrast with door, use of texture and colour, easy grip handles – 'D' or 'L' shaped preferable
- [ ] Letterbox should have wire basket to catch mail
- [ ] Avoid large areas of glazed material
- [ ] Good lighting present inside and outside
- [ ] Consider defining route from entrance door to other parts of the building with rails or floor coverings

(ii) Corridors

- [ ] Limit obstacles, such as radiator or cupboards that protrude from the wall

(iii) Activity areas

- [ ] Introduce additional lighting

(iv) Bedrooms

- [ ] Built in cupboards are preferred, again to limit obstacles in rooms

(v) Bathrooms

- [ ] Use water-resistant coverings which are easy to clean
- [ ] Matt finishes to walls and floor to minimise glare
- [ ] Non-slip, waterproof flooring
- [ ] Consider additional lighting focused on toilet area

(vi) Kitchen

- [ ] Good lighting over cooker, sink and other task areas
- [ ] Sliding cupboard doors to avoid walking into open doors
- [ ] Non-reflective worktops in a neutral colour, against which both light and dark objects will contrast
- [ ] Colour contrasts between wall and worktops, cupboards and floor
- [ ] Raised edge at front and back of worktop to contain spillages
- [ ] Non-reflective, slip resistant and waterproof floor finishes

(vii) Living/dining room

- [ ] Is there an easy way to orientate?
- [ ] Bright, but adjustable lighting
- [ ] Colour contrast between doors, walls and switches

(viii) Stairs

- [ ] Handrails to give guidance on route of stairs
- [ ] Tactile cues to when top and bottom of stairs will be reached
- [ ] Good contrast between handrails and walls
- [ ] Good lighting
- [ ] Highlighted and tactile edging to steps

(ix) External

- [ ] Contrasts between paths and parking and/or garden areas
- [ ] Check for dangers: low fences, dustbin stores, raised kerbs, overhanging trees and branches

We are indebted to Royal National Institute for the Blind for their advice on this section. For further information refer to *Improving Environments for People with Visual and Learning Disabilities,* RNIB (2001).

5.6.3 Deaf and hard of hearing

The same approach described above in relation to impaired vision can be applied to hearing. In terms of building design and specification the main considerations are:

(i) Installation of a hearing loop
An inductive loop system is a loop of wire fixed around a building (or room) which can be built in if specified at the outset or retro-fitted. The wire is connected to an amplifier, power source and a sound input device such as a microphone or lead to a television. The sound is amplified and transmitted as a current around the loop which works like a transmitting aerial. A hearing aid has a switch which, when in the 'T' position, picks up sound more clearly.

(ii) Monitoring devices
In order to help ensure the safety of someone with a learning disability an array of devices which monitor aspects of the environment can be specified. These are discussed in the section on assistive technology and include smoke and heat alarms and intruder alarms. Ringing the front door bell may fail to attract the attention of someone with poor hearing. In each case an additional visual warning is required. Most commonly this is achieved by wiring the alarm or monitoring device to a signal light, which is usually followed by lighting or flashing all home lights and/or a vibrating system of some kind. This can be a device which vibrates in the pocket or on a belt, or e.g. to shake a bed at night. The system does not have to be hard wired, instead each device can transmit a radio signal which turns on the light, vibration or similar unit. These kinds of system are not excessively expensive. The Royal National Institute for Deaf People (RNID), for example, can supply a package of a pager, bed shaker, telephone, smoke alarm and door bell transmitter and one additional transmitter for under £400.

(iii) Sound insulation

Someone with a learning disability may dislike or be unable to use hearing aids and consequently induction loops. Personal devices are available, e.g. headphones which pick up TV, radio or video or other sound via infra-red signals. However, in some cases these again may not be acceptable or useable. As a result the individual may use equipment at a high volume.

In these circumstances, or where people are particularly sensitive to noise, e.g. those with autistic spectrum disorders, shared accommodation or flats should include higher levels of sound insulation and similar design or construction solutions to reduce sound transmission between properties.

This tends to be harder or more costly to achieve in older properties where floating floors, false ceilings and similar solutions have to be considered. It may become more cost effective where it achieves other standards, for example where the Housing Corporation requires energy efficiency to be achieved. A short checklist is given below:

- secondary double glazing;
- positioning of WC cisterns;
- upgrading walls, floors and ceilings in existing buildings, quilt and plasterboards;
- soft floor coverings;
- stair noise, construction and coverings;
- door closers, quality and ease of adjustment, especially in frequently used corridors near bedrooms.

5.6.4 Sensory environments

Several of our case study projects had provided sensory rooms. In the normal course of development a set of basic skills are naturally acquired but where for any reason people do not develop these skills in their early years, or have delayed development, this will almost certainly depress their learning performance throughout life. It is also likely to affect their emotional state and self-confidence as they are confronted by every new experience. They need intervention in these circumstances. A rich sensory environment can support development, through an array of visual, tactile, auditory and other stimuli.

There are differences of opinion on how best to use sensory environments. The Snoezelen[23] philosophy, developed in the early 1980s, offers an experience in which people can relax and explore in the company of a carer. Other practitioners feel that a multi-sensory environment should be used quite specifically as a tool for perceptual development, with clear objectives and outcomes. Here people are encouraged to achieve sensory objectives and their responses are recorded accurately for use in developing individual work plans.

The imaginative use of sensory equipment can link the use of more than one sense. Whatever philosophy is applied to the learning environment, there is the potential to enhance a number of skills in a multi-sensory room. These might include:

- the development of hearing, sight, taste, smell, and touch;
- hand and eye co-ordination;
- a sense of cause and effect;
- the development of language;
- control of the environment and over events which influence the user;
- relaxation and passive stimulation;
- tools for higher-order learning.

All the above can be seen as outcomes of multi-sensory work. It seems that sensory stimulation has enormous potential for developing the perceptual systems of those who have missed important stages in development and who as a consequence have an incomplete understanding of their environment and their interaction with it.

Much sensory work involves practice in movement, such as eyes following a light source, or ears following a sound. Even those who are severely deaf can detect sound (particularly loud or low frequency sound) through the whole body. Vibration devices are often used with people who are

[23] Helsegge and Verheul, *Snoezelen, Another World* (1986).

profoundly handicapped. Stimulating the sense of touch in this way is working at the first stages of learning, which can lead to successful experience of sight and sound.

Vocalisation can be stimulated by using a simple amplifier so that the sound can be played back at an audible level. Vocalisation is not only important as a means of communication, it is also a way of improving the ability to breathe effectively. Voices can be captured on a tape-recorder. Musical instruments are an obvious way to stimulate the auditory system.

The sense of taste and smell are closely linked. Work on this early developmental skill is therefore very important. Sensory rooms provide an appropriate setting for the triangular relationship of tasting, smelling and feeling.

All multi-sensory environments are unique, but there are broad similarities. The only special adaptation to the building is the provision of white, light-proof blinds at the windows and two high-level double electric sockets at either end of the room, as well as the standard low level sockets. A wide range of equipment is available from suppliers.

5.7 Autism and design

Perhaps because autism has only fairly recently been recognised as a distinct set of features affecting understanding and behaviour, it appears to fall behind other disabilities for recognition in health, education and adult service provision. Either because awareness has been growing or because incidence may be increasing there is now a much more generally accepted realisation that service planning and provision needs to catch up. Twenty years ago it was hard to find much reference to autism in the social policy and health guidance. Now it has an accepted if uncertain place.

Autism is characterised by problems with understanding and managing verbal and non-verbal communication, social relationships and difficulty with interpreting social behaviour and therefore with social interactions. A limited breadth and flexibility in thinking, with stereotyped and repetitive activity is common. The term autistic spectrum is used to allow for this wide range of ability. Asperger's Syndrome is used to refer to a higher functioning group and Kanner's Syndrome to others with more limited ability.

There are associated differences in perception of sight, sound and other senses. Autism may be associated with other disabilities but unlike a general lack of intellect or ability it seems to be a difficulty in the way of thinking and of perceiving the world.

As the probability of diagnosis has increased then so has the need for educational services. The obvious problems that a person with autism faces with many ordinary schools and curriculum has prompted families to seek alternatives that deal with the particular deficits, giving special attention to communication and social skills.

As children get older then the pressure to think about adult services has led to new developments in supported housing and residential services but the number and range of these is still quite limited.

Problems with understanding social behaviour and communication can have a profound effect on people's ability to manage unaided even when verbal and intellectual skills might appear quite good. The question of how to manage life as an adult or a home of one's own is generally problematic even for those who are diagnosed as 'higher functioning'.

Autism is thought to put people in a difficult and confusing world, uncertain and threatening, where unpredictability and sudden change can be unnerving. In *A Guide to Services*[24] structure, clarity and predictability of the environment are put forward as the principle for design.

For those with more severe disability there will be problems such as those identified in the previous section on complex and challenging needs. For those who are more able it may be simpler solutions that are needed to make living independently a possibility.

[24] H. Morgan, G. Jones and R. Jordan, *A Guide to Services for Adults with Autistic Spectrum Disorders,* Foundation for People with Learning Disabilities (2001).

Service providers who were consulted in the course of the preparation of this guidance were asked in what ways autism services were special:

- although they were aware of the overlap with learning disability generally, there was a strong feeling that both needs and services to meet them might be quite different;
- the management and support skills required were different; a good understanding of autism was essential in planning the physical environment, the structure for individual support and general management practice, e.g. in communication and reducing stress and anxiety;
- special communication techniques were felt to be useful, such as the Picture Exchange Communication System (PECS) and Treatment and Education of Autistic and Communication Handicapped Children (TEACCH);
- a good built environment was essential for those with more severe disabilities, taking special safety precautions where people might damage doors, wiring, plumbing, plaster or glass;
- attention to individual needs was particularly important, and designing individual housing and support options;
- for many, especially among the more able, alternatives to small or larger group residential settings were felt to be under-used. Self-contained housing, either in a 'community network' or single site group of self-contained flats with the right level of support can offer both security and independence;
- those who are anxious, sensitive to noise, disturbance and erratic behaviour do not always want to live with others with autism or learning disability with these characteristics;
- people now being diagnosed with Asperger's Syndrome may find it difficult to cope in ordinary housing but were often either not known to social services or not considered to meet eligibility criteria and therefore not receiving any additional support.

An architect with a particular interest in autism, Simon Humphreys, has put forward a number of ideas in a short unpublished paper based on his experience of work with Autism West Midlands. These could be applied to large residential or school projects or to smaller domestic housing schemes:

- **Calm and order in the layout and structure of the buildings:** if a building or set of buildings are planned in a simple clear manner the user will require little effort to use and enjoy the function of the building. A clear layout, good proportions and organisation of spaces can help a person use a building without confusion as to the location of rooms and their different uses. For a person with autism, confusion is all too easy. A building that has a sense of clarity and order has a calming affect on the user whether they are autistic or not.
- **Space standards:** people vary in their attitude to the need for distance and the threat that loss of personal space induces. People with autism are more sensitive and more threatened by a want of space and react accordingly. If a building can be designed which features both large communal areas where people can mix and places which allow residents to withdraw, then unnecessary anxiety can be avoided.
- **Serviceable and hardwearing materials:** readily available and in many forms, types of materials can be specified for any requirement. People with autism can be deliberately or accidentally heavy on materials and equipment. Specifying materials or equipment which are hard-wearing and easily maintained should be quite possible but the difficulty is finding the right balance between the general use of tough materials and special equipment and more ordinary domestic standards and specifications. Learning living skills and independence means that at some stage people need to be able to learn to manage in an ordinary world.
- **Acoustics and noise:** are important in any design but people are sensitive to sound to different degrees both as a source of pleasure and annoyance. People with autism can be very sensitive and upset by noise. At the same time they can be quite noisy and unaware of disturbance they cause. Layout, sound insulation, choice of materials and furnishings can all reduce the levels of noise and sound transmission between parts of a building.

5.8 Complex needs, security and risk

Complex needs and challenging behaviour can refer to a wide range of problems of mental or physical health and behaviour that may occur together with a learning disability. It may include people with autism, epilepsy and other identified syndromes. Impaired social relationships, communication or imagination, obsessional, hyperactive, and other behaviour give special cause for careful management of support services and the design of homes.

> Risk and risk management should be part of the thinking in design. There is a useful discussion of this in two recent publications.[25]

Risk should appear high on the list of design and management considerations. Risk assessments for general management and individual circumstances should inform key design decisions. Risk appraisal needs to consider the health, safety and welfare of residents, the extent of the duty of care falling to the managers and consequent requirements for supervision, staff and visitor safety, freedom from risk and harassment in the local community.

There is a difference in the level of management responsibilities between supported tenancies where residents may benefit from additional domiciliary care and the more extensive responsibility for those 'in care' placed by a local authority in a residential care home.

In either case, the duties for managing individual risks and safety need proper assessment and planning. Some residents may be closely supervised and need someone with them on or off the premises. It may be necessary to ensure that people cannot just wander off but wherever possible movement at home and beyond should be supported or managed rather than simply confined.

[25] Alaszewski *et al*, *Empowerment and Protection*, Foundation for People with Learning Disabilities (1999); Harker, M. and Holmes Smith, A. National Housing Federation, *Risk Management in Supported Housing*, London (1999).

For example, there may be a concern about:

- safe use of equipment and fittings;
- poor co-ordination and balance;
- need for assistance with basic self care ;
- the need to control access to areas of the building;
- occasional deliberate damage.

For many people, their own confidence and ability may be such that close supervision such as this is not necessary and the aim should always be towards the exercise of choice and autonomy not control and confinement. The process of risk assessment and plans for risk management should address to what extent physical solutions are needed to reduce risk and where management methods are more important, e.g. by physically confining residents on a site or management and supervision by staff.

Managers and staff are responsible for the health and safety of residents[26] in registered care homes including:

- moving and handling – to avoid injury to residents or staff;
- fire safety – understanding and implementation of fire precautions and procedures;
- first aid – knowledge of how to deal with accidents and health emergencies;
- food hygiene – correct storage and preparation of food;
- measures to prevent spread of infection and communicable diseases;
- safe storage and disposal of hazardous substances;
- regular servicing of boilers and central heating systems;
- regulation of water temperature and risk from hot water/surfaces depending on risk to residents;
- provision and maintenance of window restrictors, based on an assessment of risk;

[26] Health and Safety Executive, *Health and Safety in Residential Care Homes,* HS(G)104 (1993).

- maintenance of a safe environment including kitchen and laundry equipment, outdoor steps and pathways;
- security of the premises;
- security of service users based on assessment of their vulnerability.

Details of registered home requirements, environmental health and fire precautions are given in Appendices 2 to 4. (Fire safety requirements are not only very important but can be very obtrusive. There is wide scope for discretion in the application of requirements which need to be negotiated and thought given to appropriate signs and the need for fire practice.)

5.9 Complex needs: a checklist

The following ideas are based on the experience of designing for people with more severe or complex needs. It is not a set of standard requirements but a checklist of points that have proved important when aiming for good standards of comfort and amenity while addressing problems of risk and safety, and avoiding unnecessary or unreasonable hazards to the daily living activities of residents or the work of staff.

Checklist for those with more complex needs

(i) Locks

- ☐ Key locks provided to external doors, each bedroom, any offices, food stores, kitchens, boiler rooms, domestic chemical stores and rooms containing electrical switchboards
- ☐ A lock system can be adopted with a master key override for all internal rooms, with a separate master key for external doors
- ☐ Separate keys for medicine, chemical stores and the office
- ☐ Lockable fuse boxes and radiator thermostats
- ☐ WC and bath/shower rooms to have sliding bolt locks which can be opened from the outside in case of emergency
- ☐ 'Push bar to open' type fittings on external doors may be unacceptable as there is a risk of people absenting themselves from the building at night
- ☐ Automatic release locks on external fire escape doors are linked to fire panel
- ☐ Any restrictions on residents should be part of a risk appraisal agreed as part of their individual care plan
- ☐ Arrangements should be in place in terms of when doors are locked, by whom, and who holds the keys
- ☐ There should also be agreed arrangements for the external security of the home and the locking of external doors and windows
- ☐ Key operated locks to the ground floor or easily accessible windows
- ☐ Use of programmable proximity card system for controls on internal access

(ii) Doors and doorways

- ☐ External doors and internal ground floor doors and corridors wide enough to permit access by wheelchair, either for people with multiple disabilities, or for access by staff using wheelchairs to assist someone recovering from an epileptic seizure
- ☐ Where ground and floor levels change shallow ramps should be provided not steps
- ☐ Doors and closers to meet fire regulations; solid core doors; doors to open against a wall if possible with stops top and bottom
- ☐ Reinforced door frame fixings
- ☐ Overhead door closers; if mechanical door closers are a problem (people try to close the door against the braking mechanism) swing free closers; magnetic door closers on internal doors wired into the alarm system
- ☐ Vision panels on corridor doors and venetian blind panel windows to allow privacy for internal rooms, wide angle door viewer on external doors
- ☐ Kick plates as necessary
- ☐ Outward opening doors on WCs, bath and shower rooms

(iii) Baths, basins and WCs

- ☐ The need to offer personal support, supervision, and training in aspects of personal hygiene requires that at least some WC pans, hand-basins, showers and baths are positioned so that staff assisting can stand beside the person they are helping; any general use bathroom or WC must provide this additional space
- ☐ The dignity and privacy of individual residents in shared housing requires that they be offered en-suite wash/WC/ shower or bath facilities where possible. Each self-contained housing unit should provide en-suite facilities, with a minimum of one bathroom and one separate WC also available for general use

- ☐ Floor drains in bathrooms
- ☐ Lever or push taps instead of cross head taps, captive plugs to baths and hand basins
- ☐ Controlled hot water temperatures
- ☐ No exposed water pipes
- ☐ Wash basins in good vitreous china, supported on wall brackets
- ☐ WCs able to withstand heavy use, option of a concealed cistern
- ☐ Baths in heavy gauge enamelled pressed steel (not plastic)
- ☐ Bathroom and kitchen floors should be tiled or a non-slip, heavy duty sheet polyvinyl flooring, welded joints, edges dressed to the wall to provide skirting
- ☐ Special baths and showers – good occupational therapist advice to avoid expensive mistakes; integral shower fittings and shower rails that cannot readily be damaged, water temperatures controlled
- ☐ Additional requirements if residents may be incontinent: for sluices and laundry facilities
- ☐ Bathroom/WC option of light switches adjacent to door outside rooms not ceiling mounted pull switches

(iv) Radiators

- ☐ Low surface temperature radiators
- ☐ Mounted on solid walls, enclosures fixed with rawlbolts, fitted if necessary with a plinth to protect pipe work and valves, lockable thermostats
- ☐ Underfloor heating as an alternative in new building

(v) Kitchens, laundry and equipment

One of the crucial differences between registered care homes and other supported housing or housing where domiciliary care is provided for the occupier is the extent to which residents will do their own cooking, laundry and other household chores. The layout equipment and safety precaution arrangements needed for registered care homes for communal catering arrangements or laundry will be very different if people are able to do some of their own cooking and laundry with assistance.

- ☐ Where residents' access to catering areas needs to be restricted, 'stable doors' can provide a useful option
- ☐ Where people have their own flats or in shared housing where residents are doing their own cooking and laundry, equipment needs to be easy-to-use domestic appliances; the microwave is a good example, washing machines should have a few programmes, not too many; a cool surface electric induction hob rather than gas; raised or wall mounted oven
- ☐ For staff or intensive use for larger groups more commercial equipment may be required
- ☐ Key switch option for power sockets for refrigerator, freezer, washing machine, dishwasher, and any electric cooker
- ☐ Non-slip polyvinyl as for bathroom floor coverings or tile
- ☐ Good quality kitchen units, strong 180-degree hinges
- ☐ Consultation with environmental health on kitchen and laundry standards and design (*see* Appendix 2)
- ☐ Electrical sockets sited to avoid long leads or cables on work surfaces
- ☐ Avoid sharp edges to domestic worktops and radiators

(vi) Communal and living rooms

Design can be important in reducing stress by providing:

- ☐ Wide corridors
- ☐ Large communal rooms
- ☐ A choice of exits from communal rooms
- ☐ Quiet areas within or additional to main communal rooms
- ☐ A choice of recreational rooms or areas
- ☐ Use of garden recreation or patio areas
- ☐ Hardwearing flooring, washable carpet or cleanable heavy use grade in communal areas, dining areas using polyvinyl, tile or well sealed wood flooring
- ☐ The layout should take account of the need for supervision and the ease of observation (for both residents and staff)
- ☐ Use of signs or colours to demarcate parts of the house, indicate room usage
- ☐ Fire appliances well out of the way, recessed in corridors
- ☐ Emergency lighting to fire officer's requirements
- ☐ Use of toughened or laminated glass (and for mirrors) avoiding large panels
- ☐ Ground floor windows which are lockable
- ☐ Upper floor windows should have restrictors
- ☐ Planned call system and possible use of assistive technology
- ☐ Telephone points and TV aerial sockets
- ☐ Furnishings good quality, robust, domestic, furniture layout included in plans for communal and individual space; use of advice and pricing by contract suppliers
- ☐ If curtains rails or blinds may be pulled down and fixings damaged, curtains may be hung on Velcro or integral blinds fitted
- ☐ Well-sited office, central if this reflects the role of the support staff or at the entrance for a warden

(vii) Bedrooms

- ☐ All adult residents to have the option of a single room of as good a size as possible with en-suite facilities
- ☐ Personal storage space including lockable space for money or other personal belongings
- ☐ TV points, phone points, call system
- ☐ Choice of good quality furnishing and decoration

(viii) External

- ☐ Flush mat wells at doorways
- ☐ For grouped flats, entry phone for office and individual dwellings, with possible addition of CCTV system, external meter and delivery points, secure letter boxes
- ☐ Light/motion activated floodlight outside of main entrances
- ☐ Parking as required (but if possible not to dominate exterior/ leisure space), the need for places needs negotiation with planning authorities to avoid excessive on-site parking for new build development
- ☐ The dustbin enclosures have a habit of becoming a prominent if unwanted architectural feature, which should be avoided if possible
- ☐ External garden/patio area, enclosed and linked to the internal communal areas and with reasonable privacy for residents and neighbours; this can be a big plus for staff and residents; careful thought is required for both upkeep, maintenance and use, the budget and responsibilities (the number of services with unkempt outdoors is considerable with keen resident gardeners a welcome accident)
- ☐ Consideration to planting and use for recreation, especially if residents are at home in the day-time or for long periods
- ☐ Neighbours (*see* Chapter 4); noise and privacy are very important for a home; who may be a nuisance or source of harassment to whom has to be part of the early risk assessment – some services (not many fortunately) have failed for this reason

(ix) Safety and fire precautions

- ☐ Intruder alarms depending on the type of dwelling and staff supervision available
- ☐ Close boarded fencing 1,800 mm, secure side rear fencing and any rear or side gates lockable and to full fencing height
- ☐ Site layout to maximise natural surveillance
- ☐ Ground floor windows tested for enhanced security
- ☐ CCTV for checking visitors or for site security in cases of nuisance
- ☐ Risk assessment in the external space such as access to main roads, other physical hazards, water or ponds
- ☐ Consult local crime prevention officers
- ☐ Individual risk appraisals to guide design
- ☐ Minimising institutional appearance internally and externally (interpretation of regulations can allow for flexibility)
- ☐ Consultation with a Fire Safety Officer
- ☐ Agreeing the requirements for an escape route, precautions, equipment and lighting
- ☐ Signage that residents will understand
- ☐ Thorough training and management arrangements
- ☐ Doors that close properly

6. Case studies

6.1 Bungalow for one disabled person living independently with support

This is a pioneering development using shared ownership to provide a new purpose built and designed home for someone who has very little physical mobility and is also severely learning disabled. It demonstrates how quality of life can be improved by working around an individual following supported living principles and that no one is too disabled to have their own home. The initiative for this project came from the family and the development was carried out by Longhurst Housing Association.

This development began with the parents of the young person who now lives in the bungalow. Their daughter lived in a large residential care home. She was clearly unhappy and had become isolated and withdrawn. Plans to close the home were announced and the parents set about trying to find something much better suited to their daughter's needs and which would provide a long term solution.

The result was the construction of a three-bedroom bungalow on a plot of land next door to the parents who live in a small village in Lincolnshire. On completion of the building half the equity was sold to the daughter who became a 'shared owner'. Their daughter has very little physical mobility and uses a wheelchair. She has very severe epilepsy and the effect of repeated seizures has been to reduce her vocabulary from about 80 words to six. She now communicates largely by 'eye pointing'.

6.1.1 Aims

The purpose of this project was to provide:

- a personalised care service tailored for one individual;
- a building and environment that would help someone with severe physical limitations to be as independent as possible; to do some

Figure 6.1 Bungalow showing porch for wheelchair access

things for themselves rather than be a completely dependent, 'cared for' person;
- a much better quality of life for the person;
- a building that was affordable within the constraints of the Housing Corporation funding regime and controls that apply to housing associations;
- safety and security, security of tenure, and minimisation of risks of neglect.

More generally this is an example of the independent supported living approach.

6.1.2 Independent supported living

'Independent supported living' is a term that has been used to describe a variety of housing and support situations for disabled people that share in common the fact that they are small scale and *not* registered care. It means:

- having separate arrangements for housing and care or support services, so the care provider can be changed without moving house;

- the focus is on the individual not a group of residents;
- individuals should be supported to have the maximum choice and control of where they live, who they live with (if anyone), who supports them and the kind of lifestyle they have;
- people should be given the most appropriate type of support for them which also takes into account relationships, both formal (i.e. paid) support and informal support.

These kinds of principles mean some or all of the following:

- people living in their own homes as owner or tenant with a direct relationship with the housing provider;
- choices and decisions for a disabled person that the rest of us take for granted;
- re-thinking of the relationships between the carer and the disabled person;
- professionals are encouraged to move away from 'doing things for' to 'doing things with';
- complexity – each set of supported living arrangements is based on each individual's needs and aspirations, each will be different;
- supported living is as much about process as outcomes.

With this approach people are more likely to become relaxed, confident, willing to try new activities. The process of involving people in designing their own services has a beneficial impact.

Residential care tends to mean larger groups of people living together, supported by professional, paid staff, frequently 24-hours a day.
The running of the home, the regime and staff practices are more formal.

6.1.3 Funding for housing and support costs

Residential care is usually based on social services funding a 'place' in a home. They contract with the owner of the home, who is usually also the care provider, for the provision of a service. While there might be individual care plans, the service tends to be broadly similar for each resident. The individual resident, assuming they are dependent on benefits, is left with the personal allowance element of any income support (about £16 per week) and if they are on a disability living allowance (DLA) mobility allowances they may be permitted to keep that. All meals and domestic bills are met by the provider of the home and funded through social services.

Independent supported living tends to mean smaller groups, or living alone, it may mean living with other people who are not disabled, e.g. having a support tenant or house mate. It does not necessarily depend on full-time paid support (but can do). It can provide the same level of care as residential care although on a more personalised and individual basis. Following the Care Standards Act 2000, it is expected that care providers will have to become registered under the domiciliary care provisions.

As a tenant or an owner the resident will be entitled to a range of benefits reflecting their status: housing benefit which will fund not only the rent but an element of services. At the moment the transitional housing benefit scheme pays for the rent, management, maintenance and possibly some level of services and support to assist with shopping and budgeting, an alarm system etc. This scheme will transfer to the new *Supporting People* grant funding in 2003.

If eligible (which means having a low or no income and less than £8,000 in savings) the resident will also be entitled to an array of income support benefits. These will include a basic element of income support plus a number of premiums related to disability. A resident may also be entitled to disability living allowance, which is a non-means tested benefit. There are two components to this, a care component and a mobility component. These are paid at different rates according to assessed needs.

The allowed weekly running costs of care and accommodation are:

Care	£1,024 (social services)
Rent	£29 (housing benefit)
Mortgage interest	£34 (income support)

* Figures correct at June 2002

Day-to-day living expenses, meals, clothing, household bills and travel are met through the personal benefits received, in this case study a combination of income support and disability living allowance.

6.1.4 Management and care provision

Although developed by a housing association, because this property was sold using a standard shared ownership lease the association has no real involvement in either management or maintenance. It is possible to amend the normal shared ownership lease to make the landlord rather than shared owners responsible for maintenance, and for people with learning disabilities this is a recommended amendment. This ensures maintenance is carried out and housing benefit can contribute to the cost of maintenance.

The bungalow was constructed under a design and build contract with a local builder for £55,000 including land. The only significant additional cost was the installation of a purpose-built kitchen by another local installer. On completion the daughter purchased a half share for £27,500. The rent is fully met by housing benefit and the owner is eligible for income support

Originally care was provided through a private care company. As the parents live next door and have continued to be closely involved in support they eventually established their own company. The company employs six staff to provide the 24-hour support needed. As far as possible a 'normal' life is arranged and the daughter is supported to go shopping, swimming, take exercise, have aromatherapy etc.

6.1.5 Funding: shared ownership

In view of the individual's multiple needs, the absence of adequate wheelchair standard accommodation and in order to enable her to live much closer to the family, an early decision was to try to build a new home. Housing associations mainly build housing to rent to those in need. Housing associations are funded and regulated by the Housing Corporation who restrict what can be spent on a property and judge each proposal according to 'value for money' criteria.

The daughter required:

- a bungalow – the most expensive built form;
- a three-bedroom bungalow – to provide for carers sleeping in although only for a single tenant; and
- wheelchair standards and special design features, adding to the cost.

This combination led the Housing Corporation repeatedly to turn down the association bids for funding to build a property to rent, the normal solution, as 'poor value for money'. An alternative, imaginative, proposal to build for shared ownership sale was, however, accepted as shared ownership takes only about half the grant required for the equivalent rented property.

Shared ownership is offered by some housing associations. It is aimed at people who cannot afford to buy outright, and works as follows:

- the owner purchases anywhere between 25 per cent and up to 75 per cent of the equity from a housing association;
- the ownership is shared with a housing association – the owner does not have to share the house with anyone unless they want to;
- the part owned can be purchased with a mortgage and for *disabled people only,* who are eligible for income support and need 'alternative accommodation more suited to their special needs as a disabled person', income support may meet the interest payments;
- the part owned by the housing association is rented from them; for those eligible housing benefit will help pay the rent.

One of the advantages for people with learning disabilities is that both new and existing properties can be purchased this way so there is much more choice available of both type of housing and place. Location is often very important to the quality of life of a disabled person.[1]

[1] More details of shared ownership can be found in N. King, *Ownership Options,* National Housing Federation (1996).

6.1.6 Accommodation

The building is a simple oblong shape to achieve the economic building required by the Housing Corporation while allowing sufficient for special, internal features. There is a small, landscaped, parking area at the front laid out to allow a vehicle to get close to the front door. At the rear is a garden which is accessed through wide patio doors, with a flush threshold, onto a large enclosed area. The parents' garden is next door and paths have been laid out to give easy rear access between the two properties. The internal layout is illustrated in Figure 6.2.

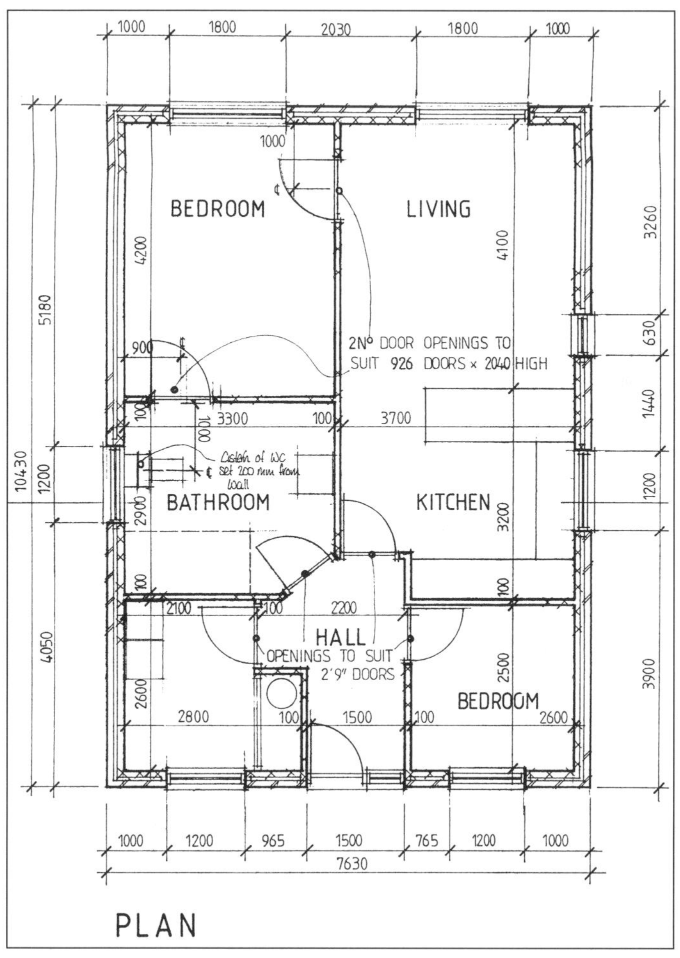

Figure 6.2 Bungalow plan

There are nominally three bedrooms:

- one large bedroom for the owner; this is equipped with a special hydraulic bed and has a large en-suite bathroom; the bathroom can also be accessed from the entrance hall which is wide enough to give a turning circle for the wheelchair;
- a second smaller bedroom for the carer who sleeps in each night; the room is connected by an intercom to the owner's bedroom;
- a third bedroom is in fact equipped with a laundry (the owner is incontinent and this is an invaluable facility) with washer and drier raised to make them easier for a disabled person to load. This also acts as a wheelchair store; like many disabled people the owner has several (four) chairs.

The kitchen and living room form a large, light open plan area for a variety of activities. In all the bungalow has an area of 80 m^2.

Figure 6.3 Kitchen area

6.1.7 Design considerations and lessons

The building incorporates an array of special features all intended either to make the owner more independent and contribute to keeping healthy, or enable her personal care to be given more easily and with greater dignity. The bungalow is mostly designed to wheelchair standards.

Parking for support workers is provided at the front of the bungalow and the ground slopes gently to the front door. The rear garden is also flat and partly landscaped to allow for the wheelchair to be moved easily outside. The area in front of the bungalow is hard and soft landscaping. It has been laid out to allow a vehicle to get close to the front door. The present vehicle funded under the motability scheme allows the owner's wheelchair to be lifted in and locked in place of the front seat. The hard parking surface has already been enlarged but still does not provide sufficient space for support staff to park and turn cars easily and safely at the time of shift changeovers. A different landscaping design would deal with this.

The front door is covered by a wide protruding porch to provide some protection from rain when entering and leaving the property, a process which can take longer than usual with a wheelchair and equipment. (This is one of the 16 requirements of Lifetime Homes.)[2]

Assistive technology includes a ceiling mounted track forming an oval shape which links the bathroom, bedroom, living and kitchen areas. To safeguard staff health, lifting and handling regulations severely limit what staff are permitted to do. The hoist assists moving the owner and is invaluable. The father describes visiting elderly care homes using other lifting devices and seeing people 'dangling from the end of a crane' – this gives considerably better dignity. The top section of the doors swing freely to allow the hoist to pass from room to room.

A hydraulic, electrically operated bed that can be raised and lowered has been equally valuable. Other technology is limited but one little device

[2] J. Brewerton and D. Darton, *Designing Lifetime Homes,* York Publishing (1996).

Figure 6.4 TV and hi-fi switches

which illustrates the role of switches, highlighted in Chapter 4, consists of two large (8 cm across) buttons, one yellow, one blue fixed to the edge of the kitchen worktop. One turns on the TV, the other a music centre, using infra-red beams.

The kitchen was purpose built. It incorporates a sink unit with adjoining work surfaces at a low level with space for a wheelchair to go right underneath. Cupboards have a deep recess at the base to allow the feet of someone in a chair to go under the cupboards so they can get close to the worktops. The built-in kitchen table made from a worktop creates a divide between the living and kitchen area. The open plan design ensures that the owner is not cut off from activity in the kitchen and can easily be seen by support staff.

The bathroom is often the most important room in design terms if a wheelchair user is to have an independent life. In this case it is entered both from the hall and adjoining room. The wheelchair can move up to or alongside all the fittings. The hand basin is wall hung so the chair runs underneath. The toilet is positioned so a helper can stand at either side and there are several grab rails.

The whole area is effectively a shower room. The floor slopes slightly to drain to a point and the floor is waterproof. The track system runs the full width of the bathroom. The en-suite arrangements work well, as does running the ceiling track from the bedroom to the bathroom.

The bathroom is very big and making it slightly smaller would have freed space for additional storage. The owner would enjoy the sensation of a bath and the track system would have made this an option. Making the whole bathroom effectively a shower room means the carers tend to get rather wet. An entirely enclosed shower cubicle would not work because of the need to assist the owner. Draining the floor to a point may not be the best solution. The alternative suggested would be a slatted area flush with the floor with a drain underneath.

Fittings and design: there are flush thresholds throughout, light switches are large pads at wheelchair height. Door handles are large, D-shaped at

Figure 6.5 Track and hoist linking all rooms showing door detail

Figure 6.6 Wheelchair access under kitchen worktops

an accessible height, carpet that is easy to clean is laid throughout. Wide doors and sufficient space in the hallway to turn the wheelchair contribute to mobility and ease of use.

A variable height sink would have been preferred but was too expensive. The sink and surrounding worktops are lower than adjoining areas and there are no cupboards underneath. The height of the sink was carefully measured to ensure the owner's indoor wheelchair would go under the top allowing the owner to help with washing up and work at the sink. The mistake was to not take account of the extra height, which the owner's chair cushion adds. The low sink height is uncomfortable for the carers to use, causing low back pain.

More storage along with facilities to charge an electric wheelchair are desirable. In addition to her several wheelchairs, the owner also has an array of exercise, play and similar equipment.

Figure 6.7 Good quality domestic washing machines raised for ease of access

The laundry is something the owner likes to help with. Washer and drier are raised off the floor but a higher plinth would make it easier for the owner to load and unload (in other cases a combined washer/dryer can be used to save space).

6.2 Grouped one-person flatlets for people with moderate learning and physical disability

This is a development of seven flatlets, some communal facilities and an emergency call system and on-site support creating a scheme similar to a traditional older persons Category 2 scheme. The model is attractive to the increasing number of people who want a fairly independent life with some support. Advance Housing and Support, the developer and care provider in this case, have other broadly similar developments completed and under construction. The architects were Tim Ralphs Design Group.

This development was completed about three years ago. It provides accommodation for seven single people, six men and one woman.

When families who have children with relatively mild disabilities that do not need intimate personal care set down what they think would suit their children, they often describe something similar to sheltered housing schemes provided for older people. The characteristics are:

- small, self-contained properties;
- warden support – someone to 'keep an eye out', to be there in an emergency, be a 'good neighbour';
- help in an emergency;
- some communal facilities and help to have a social life.

This example conforms to this type of model except it is on a much smaller scale than traditional sheltered housing which is typically 25 to 35 flats or bungalows.

Figure 6.8 The flats (showing parking at rear).

6.2.1 Aims

This project aims to:

- provide housing for people to lead independent lives with a low level of support;
- create as 'normal', definitely non-institutional environment as possible;
- offer security and help in an emergency 24-hours a day but without 24-hour on-site staffing;
- support people flexibly to meet their specific needs but to a limited extent, in practice an average of about five hours per person each week;
- help people build up a social network outside the project and do things in the community using all the normally available facilities.

6.2.2 Who the service is for

Those who live in the project have a range of disabilities. Two residents are physically disabled and have cerebral palsy, one has an autistic spectrum disorder and the others have a range of disabilities, but none of them is in a wheelchair. The residents would be considered to be mildly or moderately rather than severely disabled.

An essential requirement has been that people wish to live independently and have had to look after their own self-contained homes. All the residents now living there are able to manage their own personal care, wash, shop and make a meal. At the point of taking up a tenancy all these skills may not be apparent or residents may lack confidence and need additional support. The project is structured to allow this. Those managing the project select with care and also support parents in making the transition to their children moving on and having greater independence.

The majority of residents have previously lived in a residential college although one or two have transferred from residential care homes. One of the arguments is that this kind of project helps to ensure the life skills learnt at college are retained rather than lost which tends to be the pattern of children who return to live at home, to be looked after by relatives, or who go into residential care.

6.2.3 Funding

The building cost breaks down as follows:

Land	£125,000
Building	£220,000
On costs	£42,000
Total	£387,000 (about £55,000 per flatlet)

* Figures correct at June 2002

Housing and support costs are met from transitional housing benefit:

Rent	£69 per week
Services and housing support costs	£104 per week
Total per resident	£173 per week

* Figures correct at June 2002

All receive disability living allowance but at varying rates. Costs are met through rent, including management; maintenance and service support staff, gardening, heating and lighting of communal areas, cost of white goods. None of the residents have additional care from social services, so given that the residents are in receipt of income support and thus eligible for full housing benefit, this is an economical option for the local authority.

6.2.4 Management and care provision

The property is managed by Advance Housing and Support Limited ('Advance') who are the landlords. They provide a maintenance service which covers the structure of the building and common parts, including the array of white goods and furniture.

Support is also provided by Advance, with two part-time support workers who between them provide 39 hours support each week shared amongst the seven occupants.

The support varies according to individual needs but includes help with budgets and managing money, claiming benefits, support to get work or to take up an interest or participate in social activities. The support workers oversee the day-to-day maintenance and housekeeping of the building, meet with residents on a daily basis, help them deal with correspondence, make appointments – a long list of essential support rather than personal care tasks.

Each flat has a hard wired alarm call system operated by pull cords of the type described in Chapter 5. The alarm is linked to a local call centre which will summon help or call out staff according to the nature of the problem. The alarm has been activated by residents about 15 times over the last two years.

One of the jobs of the support workers is to liaise with each individual's social worker. It would be perfectly possible for residents to have higher levels of care provided under a contract with social services.

The present residents attend college or do voluntary or paid work including therapeutic earnings during the day. There is a Mencap Pathways project which supports people into work. Another organisation, Life Links, provides volunteers to help people with community, social activities and friendships.

6.2.5 Accommodation

The seven flatlets are organised on two floors. The ground floor also has a lounge which is equipped at one end as a kitchen/diner with sufficient space to seat four or five people at the dining table. The flatlets are laid out around a central stairwell.

The flatlets have three different layouts and vary in size from around 31 to 41 m^2, the latter figure for the wheelchair-standard dwelling while the smaller properties are to mobility standard. There is one wheelchair-standard flatlet on the ground floor.

The flatlets comprise:

- small bedroom;
- combined kitchen/dining/living room;

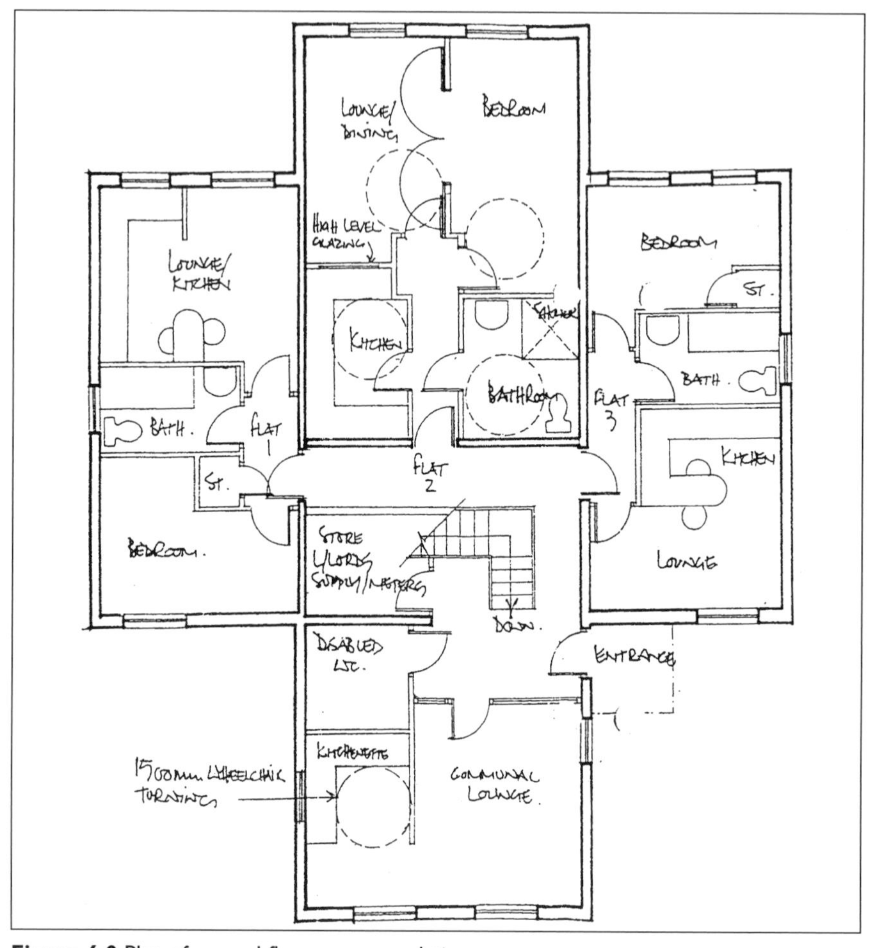

Figure 6.9 Plan of ground floor accommodation

- bathroom;
- hallway.

The decision to provide flatlets instead of full one bedroom flats was something of a compromise to make the most of the site available. Elsewhere Advance have provided larger one bedroom units and mixes of unit sizes.

The wheelchair flatlet has a larger bedroom to allow the bed to be accessed from either side. The bedroom and living room are separated by very wide double doors so effectively one large space could be created and also to make access from the bedroom to living room very easy. A large drive-in shower room, draining to a point, replaces the bath found in other properties. The usual design details required under the Housing Corporation Scheme Development Standards are apparent with wider doors, D-handles on cupboards etc.

Entry to the building is controlled by door entry and intercom system. Each flatlet is individually metered for electricity; heating is via night storage heaters. A choice of payment methods and metering is offered – payment by direct debit or using a pre-paid 'token' system. A pay phone is located in the ground floor lobby. The building is practically indistinguishable from any other private, rented, general needs housing with the exception of the communal lounge/dining room off the entrance lobby. There is also one wheelchair-standard toilet off the entrance lobby.

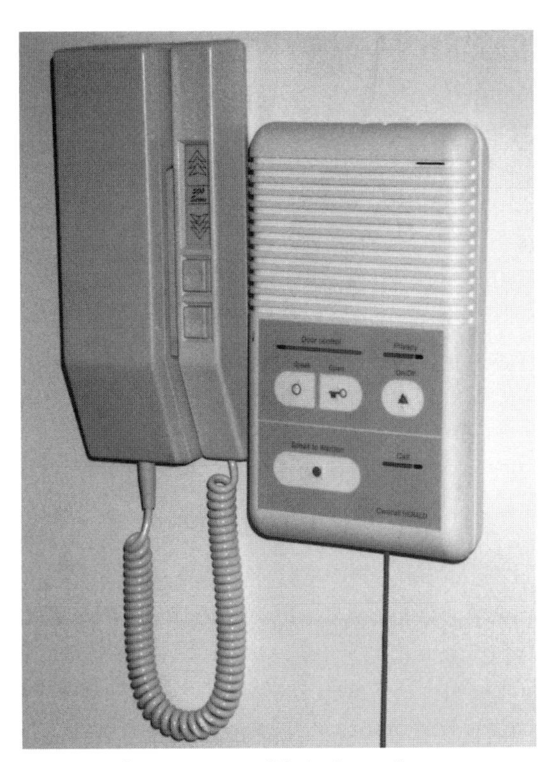

Figure 6.10 Door entry and emergency call linked to call centre

As suggested as a Lifetime Homes standard, electric sockets are mostly above skirting level throughout the building. Visiting some of the residents' homes there are a striking number of electrical appliances including music centres, videos and TVs and several residents with computers. It is clear that when designing for younger people with learning disabilities provision for this kind of equipment needs to be made, thinking through where a computer might go and providing multiple electric sockets and a telephone point.

6.2.6 Design considerations

With the exception of the wheelchair-standard flatlet, what distinguishes the overall development is the absence of any very noticeable design features. The ethos is the achievement of 'ordinary' lives and the building is a reflection of this. And yet in concept the building is at present still unusual but expected to become a much more widespread approach.

The schemes defining characteristics are:

- self-contained flatlets;
- combined lounge/dining/kitchen;
- connection to 24-hour emergency care line service – the special item of assistive technology.

The kitchens are comprehensively equipped with all the usual white goods – cooker, fridge, combined washing machine and drier. There is an ample supply of wall and floor storage cupboards. The kitchen area floor coverings are a non-slip material while the rest of the flatlets are carpeted.

Most residents have added a wall-mounted microwave and a freezer. The demand for the latter was not anticipated and thus no obvious space provided. For this group of younger people located some way from larger supermarkets in a residential area, having a freezer makes a lot of sense. It also enables relatives (or support staff) to create a supply of ready-prepared meals which are easier for a disabled person to re-heat.

Figure 6.11 Standard domestic kitchen and appliances

Electric cookers and hobs are on ordinary domestic design with an oven under the hob. This is not ideal for some of the more physically disabled and less confident, who may also have difficulties with balance. An electric induction hob mounted in the worktop with a cool surface would be safer and easier along with a raised oven. The kitchen units are also an ordinary domestic standard and not for example designed with a disabled person in mind. Both these provisions reflect the cost controls that are applied by the Housing Corporation to housing association properties.

The bathrooms are equipped with a thermostatically controlled shower over the bath. Walls around the bath are half-tiled. No grab rails are fitted and one resident is about to have some installed. Such fitting (with the advice of an occupational therapist if necessary) is straightforward.

The fittings, with the exception of the wheelchair flatlet fittings, are of an ordinary domestic style and standard. Chapter 4 explains some ways poor sight or hearing can be assisted. This building does not incorporate

Figure 6.12 Wall hung basin, emergency pull cords and support rails for WC

many of the suggested features. The resident with autism can react aggressively to noises which they find upsetting. A consequence is that they are harder on the building than the other occupants. This is beginning to tell in minor ways, e.g. damage to doors and fittings.

6.2.7 Lessons

Overall both staff and residents judge this approach and design a success. They understand and value the opportunity for independence it offers:

- An office is needed for records, confidential phone calls and meetings with residents, visitors, and social workers. At present the support workers use a large cupboard as an office!

- The building only offers the single bedroom flatlets. It was felt that some accommodation for couples would have given more flexibility for use. Site and cost limitations mean that the space in each flat is less than ideal.
- A separate laundry would save valuable space within the kitchen of small dwellings. This also provides a social, neutral, meeting point for residents.
- Each kitchen should be equipped with a fridge freezer or at least space for a freezer.
- A large garden would be preferable to an expanse of unused parking spaces. The ratio of parking spaces to flats is far too high and this was one of the requirements imposed by the planning authority. This problem is also evident in case study 6.3, where the front of the building is taken up with a large area of parking and yet there is limited secluded garden/patio area which can be an important part of the communal area for residents.
- Better ventilation is desirable and the extraction fans are noisy. People with autistic spectrum disorder can be particularly sensitive to noise.
- A communal lounge has attractions in that it provides a meeting place, space for larger family or other gatherings since the flatlets are too small for more than two or three people to eat together in comfort. It can be a place for social activities. However, in this case it had not proved particularly popular and it requires active managing. Communal lounges can be a source of noise late at night. One suggestion was that it be opened at defined periods.
- Several of the residents had some level of physical disability but some simple features found in the wheelchair accessible flat which could have been replicated throughout the building were omitted. Similarly, designs and finish details related to sensory and hearing impairment outlined in Chapter 5 were not included. These might have made the property more agreeable for those sensitive to noise.

A very similar scheme of eight flatlets has just been completed in the same area. This has retained the communal lounge and added a small office. The most significant change has been to move away from a single central stairwell around which the flats are distributed. Instead there are several entrances and stairways. This layout gives more space and is intended to give greater privacy to each resident and make it even less like shared accommodation. This development also includes some larger two person properties.

6.3 Grouped flats for people with low and high care needs

Like the last example these services provide a good alternative to shared housing, hostels or group homes. Self-contained accommodation gives more security, independence and higher standards. People can have (perhaps for the first time) a proper home of their own. One example – Seymour Court – is a scheme which provides one bedroom flats; developed and managed by Hightown Praetorian Housing Association. The other a high care service – Joshua Court – managed by Penta Hact and Notting Hill Housing Association which provides a mix of one, two and three bedroom flats in a single building.

The flats at Seymour Court in Tring provide homes for eight people with mild to moderate learning disabilities. Each flat has a bedroom to a standard to allow for two people sharing, living room, kitchen and bathroom. Two of the flats provide accommodation to wheelchair standards.

The project also encompasses a similar unit at Berkhamsted and is part of a wider network of supported housing provided in self-contained units.

Both units are close to their respective town centres, each providing ample leisure and shopping activities. In addition there is good public transport to larger centres such as Aylesbury and Hemel Hempstead.

Both are managed by Hightown Praetorian Housing Association ('Hightown'), who provide general housing, care and support across Hertfordshire and Buckinghamshire. The services have been developed in partnership with Hertfordshire Social Services, Dacorum Borough Council and West Hertfordshire Community NHS Trust.

Figure 6.13 Seymour Court flats: Hightown Praetorian Housing Association

Figure 6.14 Joshua Close: Penta Hact

Penta Housing in Barnet have a service for people re-housed from long-stay hospital needing very intensive care and choose to do this in a building which gives a mix of self-contained units adapted for people with physical and complex needs.

6.3.1 Aims

A team of support staff and a team leader are based at Tring, providing 24-hour support to residents at both locations. Both projects are funded by a mixture of rents and grant funding from Hertfordshire Social Services. Residents are encouraged to learn life skills and live as independently as possible and become part of the local community. Support and guidance is given by the housing association and other local services.

The single site cluster offers the benefits of independence but with fewer risks of isolation than self-contained independent housing. A single-site cluster gives people the best of both worlds offering a protective environment, without the loss of privacy and choice.

Service aims for cluster flats are typically:

- to help people with a range of support needs to live more independently than in shared accommodation;
- to give more rights, independence, and personal choice. The model can combine these with the feeling of living in a community and a stage towards more independent accommodation;
- to offer more opportunity for supervision and security than some of the other self-contained options.

6.3.2 Who the service is for

In the case of Seymour Court the accommodation is for people with mild to moderate learning disabilities, those who can manage reasonably well without constant supervision. The residents were identified early in the project development.

Some other services concentrate explicitly on the development of practical skills rather than direct assistance but self-contained flats in a cluster can be used for people with a range of support needs. Among the services visited there were care packages for individuals which included 24-hour on-site supervision.The limits are set between the purchaser and the provider and should be in the individual care plan agreed by social services. At Seymour Court most residents have come from 'community' referrals rather than long stay hospital, from families by self-referral or through social service placements. Hightown have provided group homes where people share but those coming from home do not always want to live with others.

The Southern Focus Trust working mostly in Hampshire and Sussex have a well developed range of supported housing services but have increasingly used groups of self-contained units as an alternative to shared or hostel accommodation and they do so for people with quite a range of support needs not just the more able.

Penta Hact in Barnet have a service for people re-housed from long-stay hospital needing very intensive care in a building which gives a mix of self-contained units. Further details are given below.

6.3.3 Funding

The local authority helped with identifying sites and capital was raised through private finance and local authority social housing grants. Eight one bedroom flats cost:

Land (Valuation)	£80,000
Works	£480,000
On costs, fees, insurance, interest, etc.	£105,000
Total	£665,000 (about £83,000 per flat)

* Figures correct at June 2002

The land was provided free by the local authority and the level of social housing grant reduces the borrowing needed, so the rent levels to cover loan repayments and other costs are reasonable. The core rent plus other services and housing support is recovered through housing benefits and ranges from £140 to £170 per week.

The cost of rent and services is met from housing and other benefits. Benefit income is higher than for residential care and housing benefit is payable for housing and support costs. County social services are responsible for other care costs met after a community care assessment has been carried out. Funding for support costs may also be available from the Independent Living Fund.

Cluster flats are typically lower risk as a capital development than shared or hostel projects because alternative use for ordinary single tenancies is possible. Other examples of more special design and higher standards and costs need to be secured against longer term agreements for revenue funding and for filling placements if they are no longer needed. The level of risk will vary depending on the balance of public or charitable grant as against market borrowing.

6.3.4 Management

Terms for occupation are usually an assured tenancy. Depending on whether personal care is provided this might require the provider to register as a domiciliary care agency.[3] Others are monitored through the annual supervision of a social services contract or individual care plans reviewed by social workers.

There are economies associated with single site management compared with self-contained housing spread over dispersed locations. Formal management and supervision is through a project manager. There are individual care plans, monthly inspection visits, a quality care monitoring system, and residents' meetings. At Seymour Court there are good arrangements with the community nurse, dietician and GP and the local Community Learning Disability Teams which bring specialist professionals together.

[3] Care Standards Act 2000 and Department of Health, Consultation Paper, *Residential Care, Housing Care and Supporting People* (2001).

Housing associations have duties towards all their tenants and through performance standards to encourage tenant consultation and involvement. Tenants' meetings, a tenant participation strategy, rules on rights to privacy and nuisance, are common practice and contact with families may also be encouraged.

A tenants' *Welcome Pack* gives useful phone numbers and local maps, tenancy agreement, information on health and safety, maintenance, staff support arrangements, visitors, residents' meetings, a copy of the Tenant's Charter, confidentiality and complaints policies etc.

6.3.5 Accommodation

The accommodation at Seymour Close is two storey and purpose built to single bedroom self-contained design standards.

The location is convenient for town but also quiet and secluded. It does not offer very much outside space, although there is a courtyard and parking.

It provides eight single bedroom flats grouped around a communal meeting room and an office. Two of the flats offer wheelchair standards. Each flat offers:

- single bedroom;
- lounge;
- kitchen;
- bathroom/WC.

Other examples visited were also provided by registered social landlords through social housing grant. All were built recently, one or two bedroom flats, with some quite large clusters ranging from eight to as many as 20 residents, although this was split into smaller units on the site. (Larger schemes run the risk of becoming a small campus and not fitting into a local neighbourhood.) Some were managed jointly with nearby general needs housing. Seymour Court is next to a sheltered housing scheme for older people. Services often had a project office or

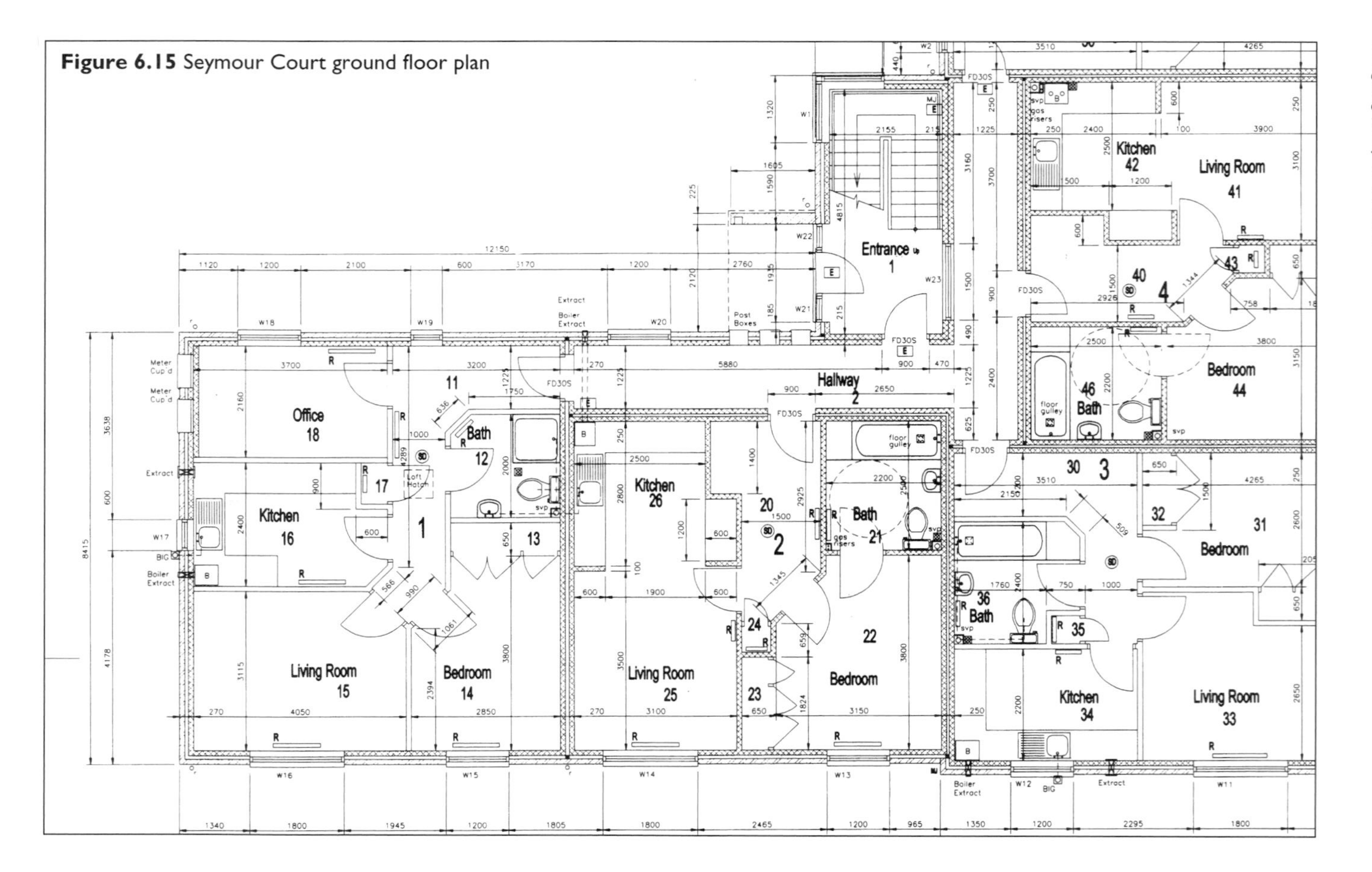

Figure 6.15 Seymour Court ground floor plan

sometimes used one of the flats for staff accommodation. There were examples of people using sheltered housing and adapting it for small scale learning disability accommodation.

6.3.6 Design considerations

These units are not unlike sheltered housing for older people but on a smaller scale. They need to allow for on-site supervision which can be assisted through the use of technology. The levels of support and supervision for residents will depend on individuals and different levels of help or care can be arranged for different residents.

The accommodation can balance the requirement for individual and communal space, bedsits with more communal living or proper self-contained flats with very little else. Design considerations will vary according to the support needs or disability of residents but these are some of the main points identified from Seymour Court.

- A high standard of specification and choice of materials allowed for greater wear and tear.
- Social services were closely involved through a project group for development which included Hertfordshire County Council, the local Mencap Society and occupational therapists and physiotherapists for individual resident's needs.
- Standards for domiciliary care were applied rather than those for registered care homes because residents are tenants of their own homes under an assured tenancy.
- Communal space and an office are provided. The communal living room has only limited use for meetings and special events and social meetings are as often in each other's flats; in other services the communal space is sometimes omitted.
- The flats are from 42 to 48 m^2, some with single kitchen/living room, others separate.
- Floors in the flats are of sealed and covered polyvinyl flooring, not carpeted, but this did not seem as institutional as might be imagined. People could add their own coverings if they wished. In another

example where floors were carpeted, the corridors were showing signs of wear after only six months.

- Equipment in the flats includes an easy-to-use washing machine/drier and microwave and residents have help as needed with household work and cooking. A cooker with low level oven and electric hob is fitted. Bathrooms are fitted with an integral shower unit or bath depending on the individual concerned. If needed, grab rails and special WCs are fitted.
- Low surface temperature radiators are fitted and hot water temperatures controlled where necessary, which is the case with nearly all of the houses visited.
- Security is not as difficult as in some houses but fuse boxes are lockable.
- CCTV is used for the front door where everyone has their own doorbell and post box and residents can check on visitors before admitting anyone. An alarm call system is used and a special alarm has been fitted for a person with epilepsy.

Figure 6.16 Seymour Court kitchen layouts

6.3.7 Mix of self-contained flats for residents needing higher support

Penta Housing in Barnet have a service for people re-housed from long-stay hospital needing very intensive care in a building which gives a mix of self-contained units. The capital for building costs was raised through private borrowing repaid as part of the overall service running costs funded from the hospital resettlement funding transferred from health. The capital costs were about £83,000 per resident which allowed for staff accommodation and high physical and space standards needed for people with physical and other health needs.

The decision to use self-contained or shared accommodation was made following consultation with residents and health staff on needs and preferences.

Figure 6.17 Rear of Joshua Close showing secluded hard patio area

Three of the residents need the use of a wheelchair but others have varying levels of physical disability. Extra space and special equipment and fittings for people with physical disability have been allowed for: special baths and shower units, adjustable levels for some of the kitchen and washing facilities, a call system, wide corridors and open layout for ease of supervision. It is a two storey development and a lift is provided for access to the second floor.

Close co-operation throughout the development phase with health and social services was vital and the individual needs received careful attention with the help of health or social service professionals. This co-operation is important in producing a clear brief. All but one of the residents had been hospital in-patients but future places in the service will be for the use of the local authority for community referrals.

The advantage of the mix of accommodation on a single site is that of flexibility in use, for people to share or live on their own, for scope to change the service over time and to arrange for a range of support needs for individuals from the staff available on site.

6.3.8 Design guidance

The design guidance for Housing Corporation funded schemes is given in their *Scheme Development Standards*,[4] which covers quality, procurement rules and costs eligible for grant.

6.4 Small registered care home

These are two examples of schemes providing a high level of support for people with physical and sensory disabilities. They are registered care homes developed by housing associations and managed by separate care providers. Each fits well within very different neighbourhoods: a Cotswolds village and the City of Leeds. These small group homes are similar in type to many others and show the value of developing to

[4] Housing Corporation, *Scheme Development Standards*, London (2001).

standards that allow for single people sharing and for the intensity of use by residents with special needs and their support staff.

Leeds Federated Housing Association is a major local provider in Leeds mostly of general family housing and on this project at Middleton they have worked with United Response, a national provider of services for people with learning disabilities or mental health problems. The architects were West and Machell, Leeds.

The house is part of an estate of general family housing provided by Leeds Federated built in 1997 specially for people with physical disabilities. The use of a newly built bungalow is therefore important because it can allow for the space and amenity needed which would be more difficult in adapting an existing dwelling.

The management of the home was tendered by the local authority to service providers and United Response, quite a large national provider, was appointed.

Figure 6.18 United Response/Leeds Federated Housing Association group home in Leeds

Figure 6.19 New Era/Shaftsbury group home in the Cotswolds

New Era Housing Association is part of the New Dimension Group, a specialist housing association working in partnership with a wide range of care providers, in this case in Minchinhampton with the Shaftesbury Society, under a similar arrangement as in Leeds where the management was tendered by the local authority. The architects for the scheme were Evans Jones, Gloucester.

The house is in a residential area, newly built on a site adjoining a larger housing association development and a school.

6.4.1 Aims

The aims typically are:

- to provide the opportunity to live in an ordinary house in the community rather than separate from it;
- to offer a lifestyle other people have, giving independence, treating people with a disability as equal citizens, empowering residents to participate in full and valued lives;
- to offer choice and participation in daily living, social and daytime activities, employment opportunities;
- to work through individual care plans, which will be regularly reviewed to see what is achieved and how things may change.

6.4.2 Who the service is for

The residents for the Leeds house all came from a much larger children's home out of the area and returned to Leeds as they became adults. The residents identified for the Cotswold home were also mostly already in services but were able to move back from 'out of county placements'. In both cases these were people with physical as well as learning disabilities. The need for the Cotswold home was in the first place identified by local families.

Group homes may be provided for people with limited support needs or for those needing constant support and care. Following the model of an ordinary home, it should be for people who want to share and who are able to choose who they live with. Then it may offer the opportunity for companionship and mutual support. Either through their own choice or by other selection process the key to success in a shared house is compatibility, a genuinely domestic environment – a home. This can conflict with other selection priorities and the requirements of purchasing authorities. The problems that arise when people do not get on with each other may have to be solved by allowing people to move.

6.4.3 Group homes

Twenty years ago a King's Fund report[5] set out aims for ordinary living using small shared houses to create an ordinary domestic scale home, which became popular for many hospital resettlement programmes. This kind of small scale was seen as an important step away from the traditional larger institutional settings of earlier services. Small shared houses give an opportunity for group living and mutual benefit for people who want to share and residents can take more responsibility, share house-keeping and other domestic arrangements.

Sharing with others in a small group can seem a positive change for people moving from a larger institution. Staff support can be shared on site and it is possible to adapt and improve ordinary housing for shared occupation. Living on one's own can be difficult and lonely so many will

[5] King's Fund, *An Ordinary Life* (1980).

prefer to share. For those with little or no verbal communication this can present particular difficulties. Small scale ordinary housing according to recent research evidence[6] shows better results than hospital and other large scale services.

6.4.4 Funding

Purpose built housing for those with complex or physical needs and learning disability need higher standards of space, equipment and amenity. This will be reflected in the cost, which can be difficult when working with usual social housing standards and cost allowances. When working with public grants this can be a problem because basic minimum standards do not necessarily allow for the special requirements of people with physical and learning disabilities. The Cotswolds service needed to top up housing capital grant with charitable and social service funding to allow for an additional sensory room and for aids and adaptations. Both provided wheelchair accessible accommodation and standards throughout.

The budget costs of the Cotswold scheme were:

Land	£65,000
Building	£195,000
Sensory room and other aids	£37,000
On costs	£76,000
Total	£373,000 (£77,000 per resident)

* Figures correct at June 2002

This was funded by a mix of Housing Corporation, private finance, local authority and charitable sources. The land was provided by the local authority which reduced the real cost and the level of private borrowing such that the resulting core rents are able to remain at a reasonable level.

[6] E. Emerson *et al*, *Quality and Cost of Residential Supports for People with Learning Disabilities, Summary Report*, Manchester, Hester Adrian Research Centre (1996); E. Emerson and C. Hatton, *Residential Provision for People with Learning Disabilities: A Research Review*, Manchester, Hester Adrian Research Centre (1996).

Maximum weekly entitlement through DSS benefits is £135.75 excluding DLA mobility.The calculation of income support top-up is £80.75 including residential allowance plus severe disablement allowance at £55.00.The rest of the costs of care and support are met by social services (between £1,000 and £1,500 a week for higher support needs).

6.4.5 Management

The project management in both services was a joint effort involving the housing provider and the service commissioner – social services and other professionals. Residents were identified very early on.The weakness in both was the arrangement for tendering the service which meant that the care service provider was not involved from the beginning.This may not be serious but their experience of managing services may be very useful and their management practices may have a bearing on design requirements.They are a major stakeholder and if possible should be there at the beginning.The omission can be costly if later changes prove necessary.

Small group homes work best where a group are compatible with each other.They can be less institutional and more domestic and informal than larger services but people need to have a choice about who they share with, or how support is provided.The management must allow for movement so that an unhappy resident can move on. Providers and social service care managers need to run services as part of a network.

The type and level of residents' needs will require different approaches to the care and support of residents. One may emphasise independent living and user control, the other be more directive, towards learning skills, for personal development or for therapeutic reasons.

A small shared scheme will have problems when lack of resources means that the service is not equipped to offer opportunities for social and personal development, and for day-time activity if people are not working. This does sometimes occur in this type of situation, but is claustrophobic in a small house and dispiriting for residents and staff. Space and design should allow enough room for staff and residents' communal or day-time use.

Individual support agreements or care plans are now used in most services to formalise the expectations of staff and residents. 'Keyworking' provides for one staff member to have special responsibility towards each resident. This encourages a more person-centred approach within the service.

6.4.6 Accommodation

Services have often used ordinary family dwellings, which may not always be ideal for single people sharing, but were readily available from existing stock. Recently, accommodation has been more often adapted or built to special standards for shared housing or to suit registration requirements specifying minimum room sizes and facilities. There are unfortunate examples of larger group homes where new build designs stand out from their neighbourhoods as being rather different and special.

In the two examples visited the houses were new purpose built. They were both for people needing fairly constant support. Because of the degree of physical handicap both have used the opportunity of new build development to provide bungalows with generous space standards.

Using or adapting ordinary housing for group homes is usually cheaper and more convenient. The housing has the advantage of being already fitted to its neighbourhood but this has to be balanced against the physical standards necessary for use and occupation.

Both houses have the advantage of a good size plot, which allows for a secluded garden and patio area which residents can use in good weather. Generally residents with learning disabilities should be able to be out in the day-time, at work, training, day service or educational establishments but being able to use the grounds may be a very important option especially for those confined to a wheelchair or for people who for whatever reason spend more time at home. Where it seems likely that residents, perhaps because they are older, are more likely to be in during the day, this has to be allowed for in the accommodation.

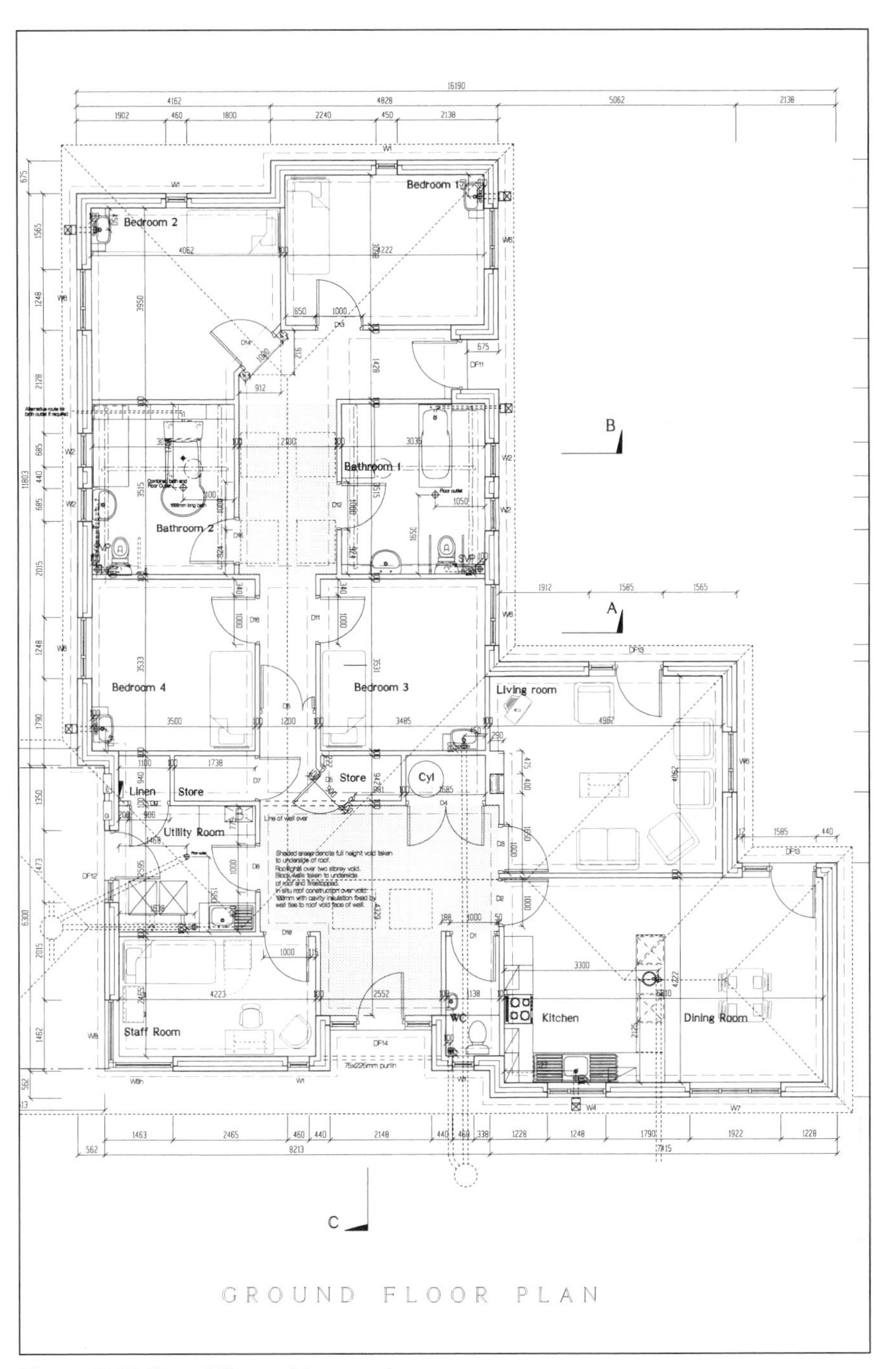

Figure 6.20 Plan of Cotswolds group home

Services may be required to register as registered care homes[7] and this now falls under the Care Standards Act 2000 and National Care Standards Commission. Requirements for standard of accommodation and management are given in a new Consultation Document on Minimum Standards.[8] Where a service is registered as a residential care home this affects funding arrangements, conditions for management of a service and occupation. Residents' access to benefits, degree of independence and autonomy is limited too.

Residents may occupy as tenants but if a home is registered as a residential care home, the terms of occupation may be a licence to occupy because of the level of management control required.

6.4.7 Project brief and development

The Leeds house was built along with a general needs estate and the scale and external appearance fits comfortably. The Leeds service was provided through a design and build package as part of the general needs development. While this may offer savings it adds another stakeholder to the long list of those involved in the project and has potential for confusing the more specialist development.

In both houses there was a potential problem over the arrangement for tendering for the management of the support service long after the scheme design and building stages were well advanced. This can cause problems but in both cases there was an experienced organisation providing the brief – Barnardo's and New Era – and potential residents had been identified.

The list of interested parties can include:

- the housing developer, e.g. a housing association;
- social service and health – commissioning the support and care service and acting on behalf of prospective residents;

[7] Department of Health, Consultation Paper, *Residential Care, Housing Care and Supporting People* (2001).
[8] Department of Health, *Care Homes for Younger Adults and Adult Placements: National Minimum Standards* (2001).

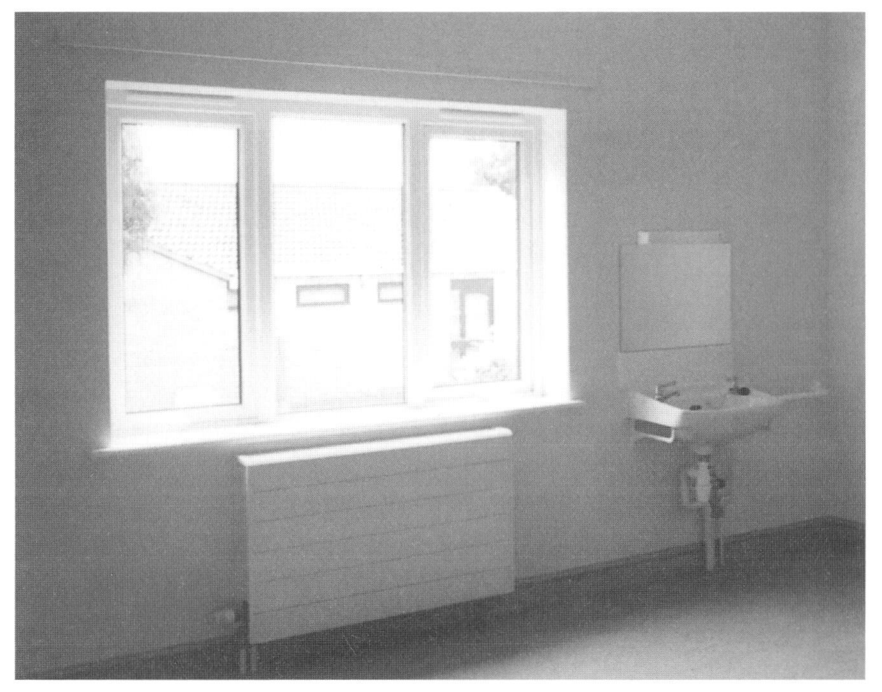

Figure 6.21 Low sill heights, low surface temperature radiator, and accessible wash basin

- the service manager, care and support provider;
- registered care and other regulators;
- and as, in one of our examples, the design and build contractor.

An observation from the architects for the Leeds service was that if possible, details of fittings and equipment, any special requirements for individuals should be left until the needs of residents and views of service managers were known. The alternative of putting in the wrong things and taking them out again is costly and wasteful.

6.4.8 Design considerations

Location is fairly good for both services, near a local centre, the village or local shopping centre, but quiet and with privacy. For hilly country, both have level sites and access and proper attention had been given to the landscaping of the land for privacy and use. Sometimes the external environment seems something of an afterthought or is omitted from the contract to save money.

Communal space is very important for group living, particularly if residents use wheelchairs. The physically small group home with higher staffing levels and people in all day can be very claustrophobic for everyone. The Leeds house gives generous allowance for communal space. A spacious hallway, high ceiling, with natural light give an immediate sense of space.

Space standards are given in the Department of Health guidance[9] for registered care homes: 10 m^2 for bedrooms and 4.1 m^2 for communal living areas (12 m^2 for wheelchair users and all new services). An earlier DHSS[10] guide suggested 39 m^2 per person in shared housing.

Personal space or privacy can sometimes feel limited in small shared housing. A place to receive visitors and private use of a telephone are valued by residents.

The kitchen design in both houses allows for some self-catering. Usually a group home will want to allow for both self-catering and catered or sharing meals. Whatever it is to be, the arrangements for catering and self-catering need to be known. Worktop heights, low level sinks, cupboard access, accessible plugs and equipment were all allowed for in the kitchen designs. As with other activities there needs to be a recognition that people are not just be looked after but helped to do more for themselves.

Equipment should follow the same self-help principle. Residents should as far as possible be able to use or be trained or helped to use washing machines, dishwashers, cookers, microwaves etc. The kitchen or laundry built and equipped to catering or industrial standards is not particularly homely nor perhaps easy to use by residents. Good quality domestic

[9] Department of Health, 2001, n 8 above.
[10] DHSS, Local Authority Building Note no 8: Residential accommodation for mentally handicapped adults.

Figure 6.22 Strong units and D handles for kitchen cupboards

machines should nowadays be able to cope. Risks there may be, but individual work with residents can try to manage the risks.

Washing and bathroom facilities were specified according to the needs of identified individuals. The alternative of fitting or making changes after occupation are expensive and difficult. The general specification of hoists, showers, baths and toilets is also potentially wasteful. The idea of Lifetime Homes, of an upgradeable design on a basic standard, is a good principle to follow to allow for future flexibility of use.

Is an office needed? The office and staff flat in the Cotswold service was out of the way in a small first floor space. In Leeds it was off the main corridor on the ground floor. The right location has to balance the need for supervision and residents feeling that this is their home – the office should not be too intrusive. It is an important decision. (At least in new build the solution can be designed but in existing buildings the office usually gets what is left over.) The use of the office needs to be known and discussed with the managing organisation when there are staff on site. In group homes some staff sleep-in rooms and work space is very poor.

Alarm call systems are fitted in both houses and acoustic monitoring for individuals because of risk assessments for epilepsy. Floor coverings – carpet, polyvinyl and wood are all good in the right place. Carpets usually need to be hardwearing and readily cleanable. A sensory room was specified for the Cotswold house but the Leeds project had also taken special trouble to provide decoration, mobiles and sculpture which would be attractive to residents with impaired vision. Some colour coding was used and residents' personal colour preferences incorporated.

Corridors and sight lines allow for ease of observation, which can be just as important for residents as for staff. For people with more limited movement it is important to be able to see what is going on in the building. Lower sill heights allow for better visibility from bedroom windows.

Parking can be problematic. Using existing buildings there is the risk that staff take up a great deal of street parking and annoy the neighbours. In new build there is the danger that planning requirements include plenty of spaces and a great area of the front of the building is prominently taken over by parking. This gives the immediate impression of a residential institution.

Heating is provided through underfloor heating in one case and with low surface temperature radiators in the other. The hot water boiler may need to be able to cope with higher than ordinary family demands.

6.4.9 Standards for residential care homes

The standards for residential care homes are given by the Department of Health and a new consultation document[11] is available from the Department or its website www.doh.gov.uk/ncsc and will be issued in due course under the Care Standards Act 2000.

[11] Department of Health, *Care Homes for Younger Adults and Adult Placements: National Minimum Standards* (2001).

6.5 Residential and day school

This is a development for children with quite high support needs and special requirements funded through charitable sources with running costs met by the education authorities. The charitable foundation has been both funder and developer. This example has special features because it is a residential school but the design issues for people with autistic spectrum disorders will equally apply to adults.

Prior's Court School is a residential and day school for children aged five to nineteen diagnosed as on the autistic spectrum who have moderate to severe learning disabilities. The school is designed for children needing a co-ordinated and consistent programme of education and care.

It currently provides places for 54 pupils and uses an existing residential school building, formerly a country house, in spacious grounds – 55 acres – with parkland and a 10 acre wood. It is near Newbury and the Newbury Showground and the M4.

The acquisition in 1998 and development of the school in 1999 was started and funded by The Shirley Foundation which has now passed the responsibility to the new Prior's Court Foundation. The cost of the

Figure 6.23 Existing Grade II* listed building

development was about £6 million. The school and residential costs are met by fees paid by local authority education departments referring individuals assessed as having the special educational needs.

6.5.1 Who the service is for

As mentioned above, the school is for children aged five to nineteen diagnosed as on the autistic spectrum who have moderate to severe learning disabilities. Autism is regarded as a developmental disorder usually identifiable before the age of three. Very simply, it is characterised by problems with:

- understanding and managing verbal and non-verbal communication;
- social relationships and difficulty with interpreting social behaviour and therefore with social interactions;
- a limited breadth and flexibility in thinking, with stereotyped and repetitive activity.

Problems with understanding social behaviour and communication can have a profound effect of people's ability to manage unaided even when verbal and intellectual skills might appear quite good.

Having said something about what autism is, it is also important to say that the common characteristics are found in individuals with a wide range of intellectual and personal ability so the term autistic spectrum is used to allow for this wide range of ability. Asperger's Syndrome is used to refer to a higher functioning group and Kanner's Syndrome to others with more limited ability.

There are associated differences in perception of sight, sound and other senses. Autism may be associated with other disabilities but unlike a general lack of intellect or ability, it seems to be a difficulty in the way of thinking and of perceiving the world. (More is said about this in Chapter 2.)

It presents special challenges in designing a curriculum, a school, the teaching and residential environment.

6.5.2 Aims of the school

The school is managed by a charity which aims to:

> Bring together good practice from around the world and form these into an approach that sustains and develops the pupil's very special needs.

The approach emphasises the use of research to test methods and develop new ideas. The school seeks to nurture and support, to develop skills and self esteem, to value individuality, to point toward independence. The National Curriculum gives the framework for individual programmes and the school makes a special effort to use partnerships with parents and professionals and to inform public awareness.

The educational methods build on other tried and tested examples including Daily Life Therapy and TEACCH. Communication is assisted using Picture Exchange, Makaton signing and Social Stories. There are communication specialists and language therapists.

6.5.3 Structures

Autism is thought to put people in a difficult and confusing world. Structures – for communication, the daily and weekly timetable, the environment and use of buildings – are very important. They provide fixed points and certainties in an uncertain and threatening world where unpredictability and sudden change can be unnerving.

In *A Guide to Services*[12] the following principles are given:

- structure, clarity and predictability inherent in the design of the environment;
- unambiguous use of language;
- calm quiet manner in working with people.

[12] H. Morgan, G. Jones and R. Jordan, *A Guide to Services for Adults with Autistic Spectrum Disorders,* Foundation for People with Learning Disabilities (2001).

The TEACCH[13] programme for education and SPELL use very structured elements in individual programmes. Daily Life Therapy[14] originating in Japan and made well known by the Higashi school in Boston uses daily exercise and group activities.

The school draws on such methods in a very organised daily programme of individual and group activity including physical education and exercise. Facilities at the school include a gym, indoor pool and sensory rooms as well as designed outdoor play areas.

6.5.4 Residential accommodation

In 1998 the first stage of the work at Prior's Court, the refurbishment of the main existing building, formerly a residential school and a Grade II* listed building, was started. This was to provide offices and administration, the kitchen and dining areas, staff accommodation and some student accommodation. Existing classrooms were refurbished and adapted. New teaching accommodation was added. An existing sports hall was divided and a new sensory swimming pool with changing rooms provided.

As well as the improvement and alteration of the existing building a new residential block was designed.

The architects were Broadway Malyan and the quantity surveyors the Andrews Partnership. There was a project development group set up by The Shirley Foundation and a very ambitious timetable set, to be on site in 1999 and to complete in that year. There were difficulties to be overcome with the first stage of the development, the timetable was tight, the head of the school was not appointed until the project was nearly on site and there were significant changes made when the scheme was under way. To begin with the plan was to be for four residents sharing but this was later amended to two residents in each bedroom of 15 m^2. These are arranged on two floors and in large domestic units.

[13] E. Schopler and G. Mesibov, *Learning and Cognition in Autism*, New York Plenum Press (1995).
[14] K. Kitahara, *Daily Life Therapy*, Boston (1984).

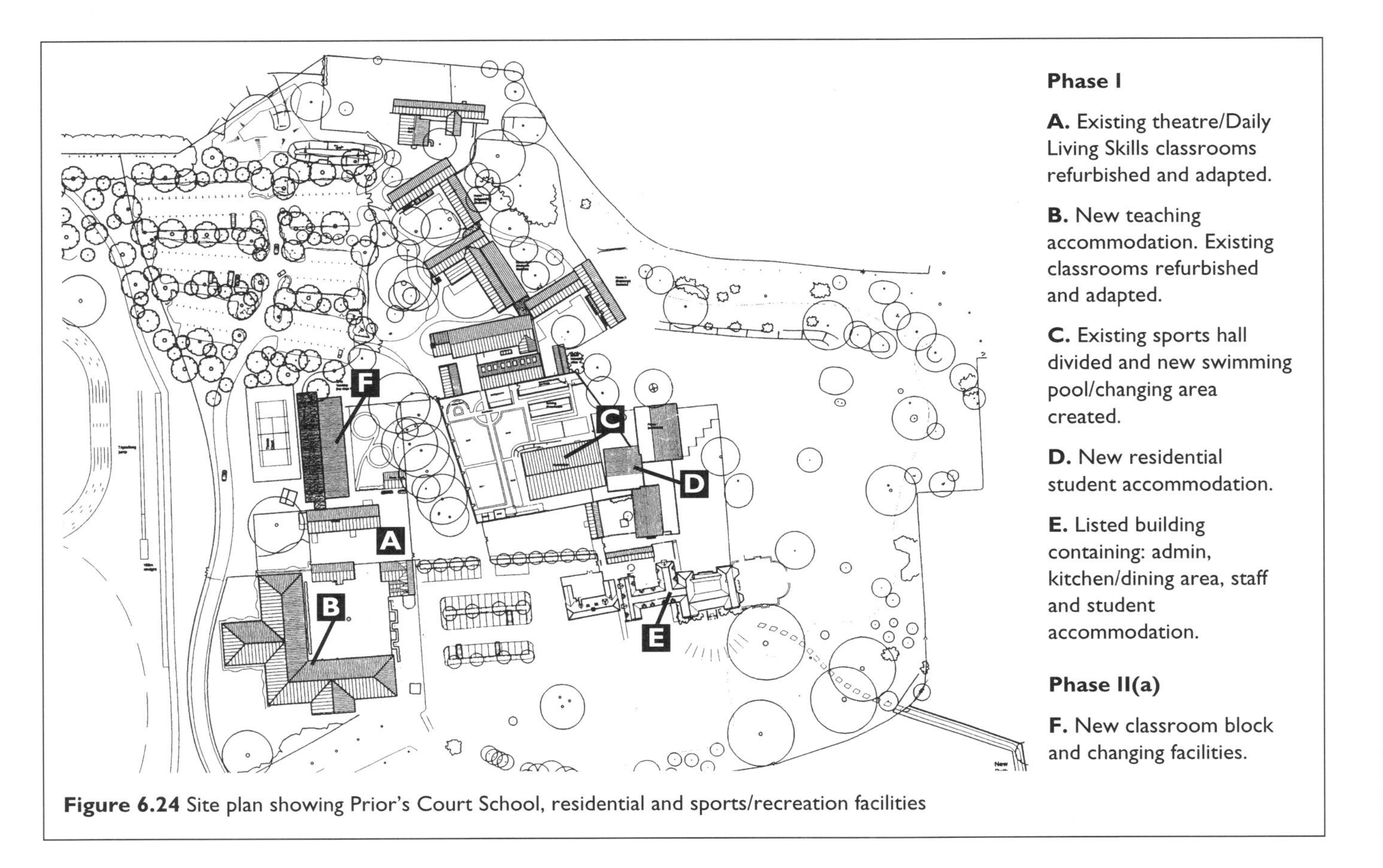

Figure 6.24 Site plan showing Prior's Court School, residential and sports/recreation facilities

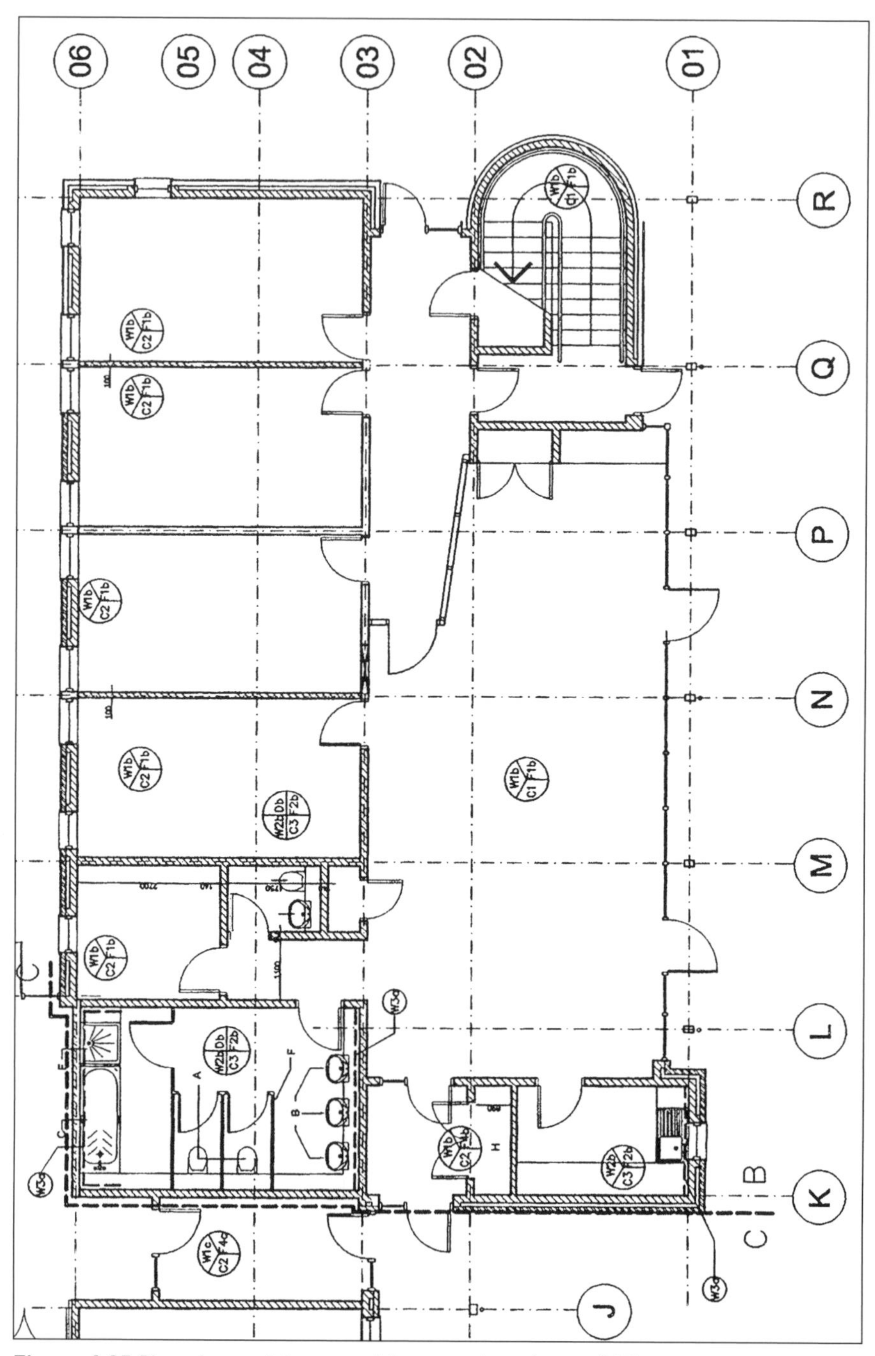

Figure 6.25 Plan of one of the ground floor residential units (Millington House).

The modern, purpose built accommodation is designed for pupils from five to sixteen years. Each house can accommodate up to 12 pupils with modern and comfortable dining, lounge, recreational and quiet areas, suited to the age of the children. Children sleep a maximum of two to a room whilst older pupils have single occupancy study/bedrooms. Key Stage 4 pupils (14+), and older live in the main house with specially designed accommodation aimed at promoting more independent living. The pupils dine as a family group using the two dining rooms, which have been designed to suit dependent and independent pupils alike. Care is provided by residential staff on a ratio of 2 to 1 with waking night staff and a sleep-in member of the residential staff responsible for pupils throughout the night.

The residential staff, in addition to providing for the daily needs of the pupils, encourage the pupils to follow hobbies, take part in recreational, social and fun activities and arrange trips, outings and special events for all the pupils in their care.

There are now plans for a second stage residential development for post-16 students. Plans were drawn up for a second group of three residential buildings planned in three large domestic units on two floors providing 24 single rooms with en-suite facilities, shower, WC and washbasin.

6.5.5 Costs

The school, Prior's Court Foundation, needed to be sure about funding for the post-16 placements and to ensure that the buildings' capital costs are affordable on a long-term estimate of revenue income from fees. The lessons from the first stage included the cost of the higher standards and facilities required for students with significant levels of disability. With two people sharing a bedroom the building costs per resident place were about £48,000 plus fees and any other on-costs. It was also shown how important it is to have the brief right from the beginning.

The first estimates for the post-16 accommodation in single en-suite rooms was roughly twice as much per person. Even with lower interest

Figure 6.26 Circulation area, first floor window restrictors

Figure 6.27 Sitting room, enclosed low surface temperature radiators

rates this is going to make calculations of a 'rent cost' for the accommodation look very expensive. If the annual fees including residential costs are of the order of £80,000, the accommodation cost is approaching 10 per cent of the budget, which would be high. The school governors had to balance carefully their need for generous space and amenity standards with building economy.

6.5.6 Special design considerations

There is a risk with autism or other specially identified disabilities that single design prescriptions or rules are identified regardless of the wide variation in individuals, personalities or levels of ability. Autism or autistic spectrum disorders cover a wide range from those who are severely handicapped to others identified with Asperger's or higher functioning autism.

With this warning there are still common factors associated with the range of autistic spectrum disorders which are worth noting.

In the case of Prior's Court School, it is a residential school. The pupils are aged five to nineteen, diagnosed as on the autistic spectrum who have moderate to severe learning disabilities. The design reflects their particular needs and those of a residential school but there are general considerations which can be identified through this specific example.

Space standards need to be generous and allow for residents' potential sensitivity to the need for personal space. Residents need room in communal areas and to be able to withdraw to their own space. Natural light is good and this gives an added sense of space.

Structure for the environment (as for the curriculum and teaching methods) at Prior's Court and at another school visited, Coddington School run by Autism West Midlands, allows for the separation of the school and residential areas and within these for different activities, sitting rooms, quiet rooms, play rooms, kitchen, sensory rooms and these are separate and perhaps identified in a special way, e.g. colour coded,

Figure 6.28 Outdoor sculpture by Elizabeth Frink: for decoration and as a location marker

and at Prior's Court by some wonderful art, so residents are clear what each is for.

Security is an issue for both schools because there is a duty to ensure the safety of children. Young children are always at risk of running off and getting lost but for those with autism the lack of awareness about usual rules and safety persist. Both schools have secure perimeters but there is also a need to teach and manage 'boundaries' and physical restraints should be the ultimate not the only solution.

Movement within the school grounds should be managed rather than controlled by physical barriers as much as possible. Otherwise there is little chance of students learning adult skills needed.

Safety needs to be part of design: attention paid to hard corners, edges, furniture, equipment, wiring, plumbing, heating and electrics, window openings, rails and banisters etc. If possible the aim should not be to have all heavy duty specification or to eliminate all risks through design, as the

Figure 6.29 Single bedroom pre-occupation, finishes and furniture

environment could seem very institutional and would not allow the residents to learn to live in the real world.

Supervision and ease of observation are another element of managing the environment and the layout, corridors, doors are important. This has to be balanced with the need for privacy and the use of technology is one way in which supervision can be less intrusive.

Figure 6.30 Use of PECS symbols on chest of drawers

Furniture and equipment needs to be simple and strong; the Prior's Court furnishings were of very good quality, solid and attractive. Special attention has to be given to kitchen and bathroom equipment and this should be robust, but not too institutional.

Floor coverings likewise have to allow for greater wear and tear and for dirt and soiling but they can still be attractive and serviceable. It depends on the kind of use.

Noise is a special concern because heightened sensitivity goes with autism and what is tolerable for most of us may be very difficult for some. Spaces, surfaces and insulation should damp and reduce echo, reverberation and unwanted noise transmission between rooms.

Sounds and music and sensory rooms are correspondingly a source of pleasure and both of the schools allowed for these, equipped with all manner of audio-visual gadgets and systems.

Communication for those who are non-verbal can be assisted by using pictures, e.g. Picture Exchange Communication System (PECS) for initiating communication, instructions, requests and identifying rooms, equipment, storage, switches, means of escape etc.

The brief for the new accommodation is now for smaller domestic units and more variety and flexibility of use for students, staff and parent visitors. The important details of the brief reflect the experience gained from the first development and correspond to those referred to elsewhere in this guidance:

- low surface temperature radiators;
- blenders on the hot water supply to baths and washing facilities;
- recessed fire extinguishers (so they do not get in the way and are less likely to be interfered with);
- en-suite facilities in single bedrooms (to meet new Care Standards guidance);
- no exposed pipe work;
- wider doors and corridors allowing for staff accompanying residents;
- non-slip vinyl flooring for kitchens and bathrooms;
- hard wearing carpeting for communal areas;
- water resistant carpet/flooring in bedrooms;
- each unit to have a living room, quiet room, kitchen and dining room;
- extra space in entrance areas, showers and WCs;
- generous storage space;
- laminated safety glass;
- integral vision panels in doors;
- programmable proximity cards for access control between units.

6.5.7 Standards for residential special schools

The standards for residential special schools are given by the Department of Health and a new consultation document[15] is available from the Department or its website www.doh.gov.uk/ncsc/residentialschools.pdf and will be issued in due course under the Children Act 1989 as amended by the Care Standards Act 2000.

[15] Department of Health, *Residential Special Schools, National Minimum Standards* (2001).

7. Summary of conclusions

7.1 Choice in housing

The aims of the 2001 White Paper, *Valuing People* are to enable people with learning disabilities and their families to have greater choice and control over where and how they live. Most people with learning disabilities live with their families. Often they leave the family home only as the result of a crisis such as the illness or death of the carer. The Government wishes to see better forward planning so that carers do not face continuing uncertainty in old age and their sons and daughters gain greater independence in a planned way. People with learning disabilities can live successfully in different types of housing, individual self-contained properties, housing networks, group homes, and shared accommodation schemes and other forms of community. They can cope with the full range of tenures, including home ownership. Expanding the range and choice of housing, care and support services is key to giving individuals more choice and control over their lives.

7.2 What makes a good home?

Service aims often refer to aims of promoting independence, choice and participation in daily living, social and day-time activities and employment opportunities. Friendships, social opportunity and community, at home and in a neighbourhood, are important to people with learning difficulties as to the rest of us. These aims have to be built into housing and support services. Involvement and participation for residents should be reflected in management practices. The shortlist of key considerations is as follows:

- choice of where and who you live with;
- having a home of your own;
- homeliness of the accommodation;
- location – for reasons of work, friends or family networks;
- living in a good area;
- good physical standards of housing, properly equipped;

- space for belongings;
- choice of furniture and decoration;
- security, freedom from harassment or victimisation;
- support and help with daily living, money management and household matters;
- accessibility and responsiveness of support staff or services.

When planning with individuals these are the kind of priorities that need to be discussed to produce the right kind of building and support service.

7.3 Providing a wider range of options

The predominant current form of accommodation for people with learning difficulties is in registered care homes. Relatively few people with learning disabilities have their own front door. Demand and preferences suggest a broader range of types are needed including self-contained housing, local support networks and clusters of self-contained housing. Single site clustered self-contained housing can have staff on site, give residents their own private living space, easily filled vacancies, flexibility for varying support, more choice and control by the resident and less chance of social isolation. Shared and self-contained housing each have their uses, and combinations which take account of management requirements and individual resident preferences are important.

7.4 Diversity

In new developments it may be possible to plan for a mix of types of accommodation, separate and shared housing within a group which allows for flexibility of management and choice for residents. A mix of dwellings on a single site can suit residents and management requirements. Another solution is the 'local support network' which links separate tenancies in a neighbourhood.

As for older people there could be a range of options, from the usual sheltered scheme with limited communal facilities through to extra care schemes with more shared and communal space. Thinking in terms of the variation in the balance of personal and communal space seems more positive than simply choosing between residential/shared accommodation or complete self-containment.

7.5 Flexibility

Ordinary dwellings most easily have an alternative use, they can be re-let or sold. So it makes sense to make the most use of ordinary general needs housing stock. 'Supported living' makes this a strong theme in its approach to services. A specially designed house may be a financial risk. Some developers have found that some large residential services cost far more than can be realised if the property has to be offered for sale when no longer needed.

7.6 Specially designed and new build schemes

Specially designed properties may be needed to provide single site clusters and mixes of shared and self-contained housing. Ordinary existing stock may not do the job. For special needs, for those with physical disabilities, multiple and complex needs, the use of existing buildings may just not be adequate. This is often the case where people need ground floor accessible accommodation or where the type of use requires special specification. Where services have to be registered as residential care homes the new proposed requirements will be more readily achieved through a new build design.

7.7 Raising standards

One of the outstanding findings of the recent research for the Department of Health on *Costs and Quality*[1] was that standards overall

[1] E. Emerson *et al*, *Quality and Cost of Residential Supports for People with Learning Disabilities, Summary Report*, Manchester, Hester Adrian Research Centre (1996).

for people with learning disability, in various types of services compared for the research, were far below that which are found in the wider community. This is true for the physical environment where:

- most are in shared accommodation;
- with limited choice of where or how they live;
- insufficient privacy; and
- limited communal and personal space.

Although there has been resistance from care home owners to new higher standards introduced with the Care Standards Act 2000, there is considerable room for improvement. Overall space standards in shared accommodation can be poor and the old DHSS 1983 aim of 39 m^2 rarely achieved. A standard of 40 m^2 per person would be a reasonable aim where shared housing is for a permanent adult home. En-suite bath and WC facilities are taken for granted for new hotel accommodation and the new minimum standards for residential care include en-suite facilities in new developments. For an adult's permanent home it would again appear to be a not unreasonable expectation.

7.8 Resident or management: who is the client?

The first point in this summary was about individual needs and choices. The concern of the recent past has been that services have paid more attention to the needs and priorities of management than residents – too 'service led'. The process of developing or improving housing has to take account of a range of views of residents, managers, commissioners, regulators, and professional consultants. Each will require access to the project planning and decision-making. Project development groups need to reflect the varying and competing interests.

This guide suggests an analysis of the balance of individual and management or organisational requirements which are then a matter for negotiation. However, social policy and forms of support for adults with learning disabilities have clearly been moving toward ordinary homes and away from institutions.

A critical part of this is that residents for any proposed housing project should be identified at an early stage so that the planning process can take account of any special needs or wishes. To give people a real choice they either have to be able to decide whether they want to live in the accommodation provided or not, or the commissioning organisation should act as advocate for their needs.

Three important elements of early planning are:

- identifying residents and their particular needs and giving them a choice in where they live and with whom;
- deciding on the structure for management and support for residents;
- deciding how ordinary or special the design should be;
- providing a home which is located in a community with access to neighbourhood services.

7.9 Regulation

Regulation can have an unfortunate impact on building design and attention should concentrate at an early stage on the likely extent of regulation requirements, for planning permission, fire precautions, standards for homes in multiple occupation and registration under the Care Standards Act 2000, in order to minimise unwanted effects.

7.10 Location

The location of the site or building is of critical importance. In choosing what is suitable it is important to:

- ensure accessibility to shops and local facilities, transport links, job opportunities and day centres;
- make an appraisal of possible problems or issues in the location of a new building in a neighbourhood, avoiding social isolation;

- take account of residents' friendship and neighbourhood networks;
- provide safety, security and freedom from harassment; avoid concentrations of special services and multiple occupation.

7.11 New ideas for the use of technology

Some of the difficulty of designing for people with learning disabilities is reconciling the need for independence and privacy with a requirement for safety and supervision. In services for older people the idea of using alarms, call systems, automatic warnings, a whole array of electronic communications has given the possibility of less intrusive safety measures. This is also beginning to find its place in housing for people with learning difficulties.

8. Appendices

Appendix 1. Planning permission

Planning permission has caused problems for several reasons; it may not be clear when permission is required; local authority policy over single person shared housing may not be explicit; and the criteria which are applied may vary widely across the country. The legislation and terms used are open to different interpretations and cases must serve as a guide. It may be necessary to seek advice on interpretation.

The Town and Country Planning Act 1990 is the principal Act which covers the control of new development. Section 55 of the 1990 Act defines the meaning of 'development' and defines whether planning permission is required; section 64 allows for anyone proposing to carry out work to apply for a determination as to whether or not planning permission is required. The Department of the Environment Circular 13/87, *Changes of Use of Buildings and Other Land: The Town and Country Planning (Use Classes) Order 1987* and a 1994 amendment are intended to clarify the position. The Town and Country Planning (Use Classes) Order 1987 No 764 has the following definitions:

- Class C1: Hotels and boarding houses: use as a boarding or guest house or as a hotel where, in each case, no significant element of care is provided.
- Hostel: since 1994, hotels and boarding houses (C1) have been separated from hostels, so change of use will apply between the two categories. Hostel is broadly defined as non self-contained residential accommodation with board or facilities for preparation of food.
- Class C2: Residential institutions, this comprises:
  - use for the provision of residential accommodation and care to people in need of care (other than a use within class C3 (dwelling-houses));
  - use as a hospital or nursing home;
  - use as a residential school, college or training centre.

- Class C3: Dwelling-houses, this comprises:
  – use as a dwelling-house (whether or not as a sole or main residence);
  – by a single person or by people living together as a family; or
  – by not more than six residents living together as a single household (including a household where care is provided for residents).*

*Where 'care' means personal care for people in need of such care by reason of old age, disablement, past or present dependence on alcohol or drugs or past or present mental disorder, and in class C2 also includes the personal care of children and medical care and treatment.

In summary there is some confusion still on what is a C2 and C3 home – in both care may be provided, but a small residential care home and a household where care is provided are not clearly distinguished, nor does the need to register under the Registered Homes Act 1984 distinguish them.

We would propose that small homes should however be treated as C3 unless advised otherwise.

Conditional permissions

The planning authority in granting permission is able to place conditions on the consent. However, certain types of condition which have been granted in the past are not justified and may be unacceptable to the Housing Corporation or other organisation providing finance for the scheme.

Appendix 2. Environmental health requirements

Environmental health requirements are designed to ensure that in houses in multiple occupation (HMOs) the amenities are provided to a reasonable standard. The legislation has now been consolidated in the Housing Act 1985 but dates originally from the Housing Act 1957. This introduced the concept of 'unfitness' which could be applied to 'a house let in lodgings'. In addition to specifying the standard of amenities, environmental health legislation also exists to ensure proper standards of management in HMOs, to require adequate means of escape in case of fire (*see* Appendix 3), to prevent overcrowding or to make a 'control order' on an HMO or part of an HMO.

What is a house in multiple occupation?

The phrase used to define an HMO used in the Housing Act 1985 (section 345) is that the house is 'occupied by persons who do not form a single household'.

Until recently the most important guide on this was the decision in *Simmons* v *Pizzey* ([1979] AC 37) in the House of Lords which gave the following points as guidance on interpretation:

- whether the size of the group is such that it could reasonably be regarded as a household in the area;
- the fluctuating character and fortuitous relationships of the group or its durability;
- whether there is a permanent community, not a temporary refuge for individuals.

In *Barnes* v *Sheffield City Council* ([1995] 27 HLR 719), the Court of Appeal considered whether a group of students living in a shared house were a single household. The Court said that although it would be wrong to suggest that there was a litmus test which could be applied to the question whether there were separate households, the following factors were helpful indicators:

- whether the persons living in the house came to it as a single group or whether they were independently recruited;
- what facilities were shared;
- whether the occupiers were responsible for the whole house or just their rooms;
- whether individual tenants were able to, or did, lock other occupiers out of their rooms;
- whose responsibility it was to recruit new occupiers when individuals left;
- who allocated rooms;
- the size of the property;
- how stable the group composition was;
- whether the mode of living was communal.

The decision of the county court judge that the house was not an HMO because the group of students occupying it were a single household was upheld.

What amenities does the legislation cover?

The net of the legislation is extremely wide. Sections 352–357 of the Housing Act 1985 enable the local authority to serve notices on the person in control of the house about standards of the following:

- natural and artificial lighting;
- ventilation;
- water supply and personal washing facilities;
- facilities for the storage, preparation and cooking of food and for the disposal of waste water;
- installations for space heating or the use of space heating appliances;
- overcrowding.

Appendix 3. Building Regulations and fire precaution standards

Fire precautions are covered by a number of pieces of legislation and guidance: the Care Standards Act 2000, Housing Act 1985, Fire Precautions Act 1971, Housing and Building Control Act 1984, Department of Environment Circular 12/92, Houses in Multiple Occupation: Guidance to Local Authorities on Standards of Fitness under Section 352 of the Housing Act 1985 and Building Regulations.

Fire Precautions Act 1971

This Act principally relates to hotels and boarding houses and will therefore apply to only a very few shared housing schemes. The Act is enforced by the fire authority for the area and requires that the relevant premises must have a fire certificate.

Housing and Building Control Act 1984

This Act introduced the system of building regulations which apply to the whole country. The Building Regulations 1991 No 2768 incorporate means of escape requirements. There are also three sets of guidance on standards issued by the Home Office or Department of Health.

- Home Office/Department of Environment, *Guide to Means of Escape and Related Fire Safety Measures in Certain Existing Houses in Multiple Occupation.*
- DHSS, *Guide to Fire Precautions in NHS Housing in the Community for Mentally Handicapped (or Mentally Ill) People,* Health Technical Memorandum 88 (1986), for health care premises not more than two storeys for residents not requiring overnight supervision.
- Home Office, *Draft Guide to Fire Precautions in Existing Residential Care Premises* (1983), giving standards for registered homes.

Houses in multiple occupation

National guidance for fire regulations for shared housing, hostels, and self-contained housing appears in Department of Environment Circular 12/92, *Houses in Multiple Occupation: Guidance to Local Authorities on Standards of Fitness under Section 352 of the Housing Act 1985,* covering means of escape, fire fighting equipment, fire instructions, drills and notices, fire detection equipment and building standards.

The part of the 1984 Act relating to houses in multiple occupation allows a local authority, or in cases where the Secretary of State makes it mandatory, compels a local authority to use its powers following consultation with the fire authority to:

- order work to be done to provide adequate fire escapes;
- close part of the house; or
- accept an undertaking that part of the house will not be used for habitation.

In order to allow this work to be carried out, local authorities may make a special grant and in certain circumstances, the provision of such a grant is mandatory.

The standards for fire precaution measures in a small shared housing scheme are different from ordinary family housing. Shared housing schemes require measures to be taken:

- to provide protection of parts of the premises to enable occupiers of that part to stay secure until they are rescued;
- to provide a separate means of escape for occupiers to leave quickly and safely;
- to provide for the detection of a fire through a fire alarm system.

Furniture and Furnishings (Fire) (Safety) Regulations 1988 No 1324 (as amended 1989)

These Regulations set new levels of fire resistance for domestic upholstered furniture, furnishings and other products containing upholstery.

Fire Precautions (Workplace) Regulations 1997 No 1840 (as amended 1999)

These Regulations require employers to carry out a fire risk assessment of the workplace:

- identify the significant findings of the risk assessment and the details of anyone who might be especially at risk in case of fire (these must be recorded if more than five people are employed);
- provide and maintain such fire precautions as are necessary to safeguard those who use the workplace;
- provide information, instruction and training to employees about the fire precautions in the workplace.

Care Standards Act 2000

Registration as a registered home under this Act will only be granted if the fire detection and prevention measures are adequate, as advised by the fire officer. Homes need a fire certificate and the requirements now appear in the Building Regulations 1991.

Appendix 4. Care Standards Act 2000: National Minimum Standards for Care Homes for Younger Adults

The following is an extract of key points.

Environment

Service users live in a homely, comfortable and safe environment. Minimum total average living space (bedroom and communal space) of 14.1 m^2 (17.1 m^2 for wheelchair users).

New homes: maximum of 20 people with no more than ten sharing a staff group, a dining area and other common facilities. Existing, larger homes to be on this basis by 2007.

The home offers access to local amenities, local transport and relevant support services as appropriate.

The premises are fully accessible to all service users; homes accommodating wheelchair users provide level access and 800 mm doorways throughout.

The premises meet the requirements of the local fire service and environmental health department, health and safety and Building Acts and Regulations, and from 2004 the Disability Discrimination Act 1995, Part 3.

Individual rooms

These should suit needs and lifestyles and promote independence. All residents are offered the option of single room, shared rooms are to be phased out by 2004 unless people want to continue to share.

Single rooms in current use have at least 10 m^2 usable floor space (from 1 April 2007), or at least 9.3 m^2 if compensatory space (en-suite facility or additional communal space for private use) is provided.

Single rooms in current use accommodating wheelchair users and service users with complex nursing needs (e.g. ventilation/life support systems) have at least 12 m^2 (excluding any en-suite) .

New build registrations provide individual en-suite bedrooms with at least 12 m^2 usable floor space (except for placements for less than three months) excluding en-suite.

Service users' own rooms include:

- bed, table, chest of drawers and two comfortable chairs;
- wardrobe/cupboard space and lockable storage space;
- wash hand basin (unless en-suite);
- space for service users' possessions;
- two double sockets, TV aerial point, and telephone point;
- bedding, curtains and floor covering;
- window which opens, at a level providing a view when seated;
- lighting and individually controlled heating;
- choice of furniture and decoration;
- lockable bedroom doors.

Toilets and bathrooms

In existing homes, en-suite toilets and wash basins where possible.

- WCs shared by no more than three people by 2004 and bathrooms by three;
- WCs and bathrooms are adjacent to service users' bedrooms;
- WCs and bathrooms to be lockable.

In new registrations en-suite toilets and hand basins to be provided or a minimum of one WC and bath/shower for every two residents.

Shared space

For shared and private use:

- outdoor space proportionate to number of service users and staff on duty;
- domestic scale kitchen and laundry;
- baths/showers (lockable);
- communal areas (e.g. for meals, social activities) of at least 4.1 m^2 per service user, 5.1 m^2 per service user with wheelchair/mobility aids;
- a private area for e.g. visitors, consultations or treatment;
- a separate smoking area if the home does not have a 'no smoking' policy.

Staff are provided with adequate facilities including for sleeping in.

Adaptations and equipment

These should maximise independence. Homes offering a service to people with physical disabilities provide specialist equipment as needed, for example:

- moving equipment/overhead tracking for hoists;
- stair rails, lifts;
- environmental control system;
- appropriate bathroom fittings/equipment;
- call alarm systems;
- lowered light switches, work surfaces, window openings;
- storage/recharging facilities for wheelchairs/mobility equipment.

Homes offering a service to people with sensory impairment provide specialist aids and adaptations:

- loops/microphones/minicoms/textphones/videophone;
- additional and/or anti-glare lighting; colour contrasting; tactile symbols; varied textural surfaces;
- fluorescent or padded hazards/obstructions (where they cannot be removed);

- computer for users' personal use;
- TV with video recorder and subtitling facility/sign language.

Provision of aids, adaptations and equipment follows assessment by, and meets the recommendations of, an occupational therapist or other suitably qualified specialist.

Safety systems and equipment are appropriate for people with mobility/ sensory problems, e.g. flashing light fire alarms, magnetic fire doors.

Hygiene and control of infection

The home is clean and hygienic. Laundry facilities are sited so that soiled articles, clothing and infected linen are not carried through areas where food is stored, prepared, cooked or eaten.

Washing machines have the specified programming ability to meet disinfection standards.

Services and facilities comply with the Water Supply (Water Fittings) Regulations 1999 No 1148.

Health and safety of residents and staff

Managers are responsible for health and safety of residents and staff including:

- moving and handling: to avoid injury to residents or staff;
- fire safety: understanding and implementation of fire precautions and procedures;
- first aid: knowledge of how to deal with accidents and health emergencies;
- food hygiene: correct storage and preparation of food;
- measures to prevent spread of infection and communicable diseases;
- safe storage and disposal of hazardous substances;
- regular servicing of boilers and central heating systems;
- regulation of water temperature and risk from hot water/surfaces depending on risk to residents;

- provision and maintenance of window restrictors, based on an assessment of risk;
- maintenance of a safe environment including kitchen and laundry equipment, outdoor steps and pathways;
- security of the premises;
- security of service users based on assessment of their vulnerability.

There must be compliance with relevant legislation including:

- Health and Safety at Work Act 1974;
- Management of Health and Safety at Work Regulations 1999 No 3242;
- Workplace (Health, Safety and Welfare) Regulations 1992 No 3004;
- Provision and Use of Work Equipment Regulations 1992 No 2932;
- Electricity at Work Regulations 1989 No 635;
- Health and Safety (First Aid) Regulations 1981 No 917;
- Control of Substances Hazardous to Health Regulations (COSHR) 1988 No 1657;
- Manual Handling Operations Regulations 1992 No 2793;
- Reporting of Injuries, Diseases and Dangerous Occurrences Regulations (RIDDOR) 1995 No 3163.

Appendix 5. Accessibility: Scheme Development Standards

See the Housing Corporation, *Scheme Development Standards* (2001).

External and internal environments should provide access for user groups and visitors with limited mobility.

Tests of compliance-essential items:

Approach to the dwelling:

- paths slip-resistant and smooth, 900 mm wide, maximum cross falls 1:40, shallow crossings;
- ramps maximum 5 m at 1:12 or maximum 10 m at 1:15;
- protected edges to pathways where higher than adjoining levels;
- entrance landing, nominally level, minimum 1.2 m x 1.2 m (inward opening door);
- unavoidable steps (not to occur within ramps), maximum riser 150 mm, minimum going 280 mm;
- paths protected with handrail where adjacent drop in level exceeds 380 mm;
- contrasting textures or kerb used to distinguish between foot and vehicular access;
- dropped kerbs used at roadway crossings;
- path gateways provide minimum 850 mm clear opening (no step at gateway).

Main entrance to the dwelling (including main entrance from communal lobby or landing):

- clear opening minimum 850 mm;
- nominally flat threshold (maximum upstand 15 mm).

Other doorways:

- secondary external doors minimum 750 mm clear openings;
- internal doors minimum 750 mm clear openings (wider where turning from 900 mm passage).

Ground floor passageways (includes upper floor units accessed by communal lift):

- passage widths minimum 900 mm generally (750 mm where intrusions, e.g. radiators);
- where turning into 750 mm doorway, area of wider passageway provided;
- where 90° turn, protruding corner splayed or one passageway 1,200 mm wide.

Entrance level WC and basin provided (all units).

Staircase suitable for future RS stair-lift, in terms of width and top and bottom landings?

Tests of performance, recommended items:

- accessible paving outside external door;
- all external doors wheelchair accessible;
- ground floor WC is fully wheelchair accessible;
- living room situated at entrance level;
- in dwellings of more than one storey, a ground floor space could be used as a bed space;
- adequate space for turning of a wheelchair in kitchens, dining areas and living rooms;
- stair configuration: full flight at 35 pitch or half landing within a stair of 42 pitch;
- door handles, switches and thermostats, etc. set between 900–1,200 mm above floor;
- socket outlets set between 450–600 mm above room floor level.

Full accessibility and ease of manoeuvrability should be provided in environments designed for use by wheelchair users.

Tests of compliance, essential items:

Moving around outside:

- paths slip-resistant and smooth, 1,200 mm wide, maximum cross falls 1:40, shallow crossings;
- ramps maximum 5 m at 1:12 or maximum 10 m at 1:15;
- protected edges to pathways where higher than adjoining levels.

Using outdoor spaces:

- path gateways provide minimum 850 mm clear opening;
- accessible paving outside external door;
- accessible clothes drying facilities;
- accessible route from external door, external storage and external gate.

Approaching the home:

- slip-resistant smooth paved area minimum 5.4 m x 3.6 m, covered at a height of 2.2 m;
- accessible route to entrance;
- entrance landing, nominally level, minimum 1.5 m x 1.5 m;
- canopy minimum 1.2 m x 1.2 m set at maximum height 2.3 m;
- lighting to transfer space, route and entrance with PIR (Pyroelectric infra-red) detectors and internal switching.

Negotiating the entrance door:

- clear opening minimum 800 mm, relevant approach space, accessible threshold;
- suitably positioned: secure lock, latch with lever pull handles, or remote system;

- suitable provision for future installation of remote controlled door opener.

Entering and leaving, dealing with callers:

- clear space upon entering for transfer to second chair;
- adjacent storing and charging of wheelchair, turning space minimum 1.5 m x 1.2 m;
- suitably positioned: post collector and provision for future installation of entry phone.

Negotiating the secondary door:

- external nominally level landing minimum 1.5 m x 1.5 m;
- clear opening minimum 800 mm, relevant approach space, accessible threshold;
- suitably positioned: secure lock (or multi-locking), pull handles and stays;
- external lighting to door and routes with PIR detectors and internal switching.

Moving around inside/storing things:

- all passage widths minimum 900 mm;
- where 90° turn, protruding corner splayed or one passageway 1.2 m wide;
- where 180° turn necessary, passageway 1.5 m wide;
- clear door opening minimum 775 mm, relevant approach and operating space;
- storage depth and width, in combination with shelving layout, provides suitable access.

Moving between levels:

- where required: lift to BS5900 (1991), full range of safety features, space to use?

Using living spaces:

- extra space for wheelchair user to circulate, transfer, use furniture and operate fittings.

Using the kitchen:

- extra space, suitable worktop and fitting layout for practical use by a wheelchair user;
- clear manoeuvring area minimum 1.8 m x 1.4 m;
- kitchen storage in a position and format which is largely wheelchair user accessible;
- built-in hob and oven, extra serviced spaces for three appliances (or four in five person plus units);
- all controls and socket outlets accessible, remote and labelled switching as required;
- suitable internal refuse arrangements manageable from wheelchair.

Using the bathroom:

- extra space in bathroom for both bath and shower with at least one to be fully installed (individual dwellings);
- extra space in bathroom for both bath and shower with 'wheel-in' shower fully installed (schemes with separate assisted bathing facilities);
- shower area is wheelchair accessible with floor drain;
- where bath installed, defined wheel-in shower space with fitted floor drain provided (all);
- Four person plus units: second WC provided with opposite hand transfer arrangement to main WC;
- layout ensures independent approach, manoeuvre, transfer and use of all fittings;
- suitable positioning of fittings to baths and WCs, fittings selected for ease of operation.

Using bedrooms:

- extra space to ensure wheelchair user access to beds, furniture, fittings and facilities;
- adjacent to bedhead: socket outlets, TV/FM points, two-way light, entry phone point;
- main bedroom to bathroom connected by full height knock-out panel, or other means;
- suitable provision for future hoist to run between main bedroom and bathroom.

Operating doors:

- door construction suitable for subsequent fixing of pulls or other fittings;
- all doors have suitably positioned, easily operated handles, pulls, etc.;
- inward opening doors to bathrooms/WC/showers openable in emergency from outside;
- any self-closing doors used are capable of independent operation by wheelchair user.

Operating windows:

- opening and ventilation controls operable by wheelchair user (manual/geared/power);
- windows opening over paths do not create hazards;
- glazing line in living/dining/bedrooms no higher than 810 mm above room floor level;
- full width transoms avoided in window areas below 1.5 m above room floor level.

Controlling services:

- suitable control of mains water stopcock, gas and electric main consumer units;
- suitable isolating valves to sink, washing machine, WC, etc.;
- flexible plumbing to adjustable fittings, where provided;

- low surface temperature radiators in restricted areas;
- suitable electrical and heating control fittings provided;
- suitable provision of personal alarms and for smoke alarms;
- suitable provision for future telephone and intruder alarm installation.

Appendix 6. The role of social services, health and housing authorities

Social services authorities are the lead agency for planning and arranging community care. Their responsibilities include:

- preparing a community care plan which describes their plans to address community care needs within their area and joint investment plans with health authorities for learning disability services;
- undertaking assessments of any individual who may have a need for community care services;
- involving health and housing authorities, service users, carers and the independent sector in plans and in planning care for individuals;
- funding for community care placements.

Housing authorities are responsible for developing housing strategies that address the full range of housing needs in their area and make the best use of the private, public and voluntary sector housing stock. Housing authorities are expected to co-operate with social services authorities in implementing community care by:

- contributing to the development of joint policies and joint investment plans for learning disabilities;
- making available a range of housing advice and services;
- taking full account of individuals' needs when allocating tenancies; and
- making investment decisions and priorities based on a proper assessment of the future needs of the local population.

Housing authorities in preparing housing strategies should consult social services and take account of needs identified through the community care planning process. Housing providers, including local authorities and other social landlords, have a key role in making suitable housing available to vulnerable people. They may also be involved in providing support and care services to individuals, with funding from their own resources, or from social services, health agencies or other sources.

Section 167 of the Housing Act 1996 requires local housing authorities, through their allocations policy, to ensure that reasonable preference is given to certain priority need categories, and additional preference to those with a particular need for settled accommodation on medical or welfare grounds, who cannot reasonably be expected to find accommodation for themselves in the foreseeable future.

Health authorities remain a major funder of accommodation and support, spending nearly as much as the local authority on adult services. The guidance of the 2001 White Paper requires health and social services to plan together through partnership boards producing joint investment plans for learning disability.[1]

The Housing Corporation distributes central government housing capital and revenue resources to registered social landlords, regulates their housing activities including ensuring their continued viability, and seeks to promote innovation and good practice. The Corporation works with local authorities on the identification of local needs, and follows housing authorities' priorities in allocating capital funding for new developments. The Corporation also works with housing authorities to seek the views of relevant agencies (including social services) when reviewing revenue funding for special needs schemes.

Registered social landlords or housing associations have a crucial role as developers working with the Housing Corporation and local authority. They can act as developers using both public and private finance and there is an established track record in providing buildings, housing management and support services. They may also provide care services directly or sometimes in partnership with care providers which may be specialist organisations and charities, or social services and care trusts.

[1] Department of Health, Circular HSC 2001/016 LAC(2001)23, *Valuing People: Implementation Guidance* (2001); Department of Health, *Joint Investment Plans: A learning Disability Workbook* (2001).

There are well established structures for these partnerships to ensure proper accountability and the introduction of new *Supporting People* grants will take this framework for partnership forward.

Structure for joint working

Guidance from the Department of Health/Department of Environment, Transport and the Regions in 1997, *Housing and Community Care: Establishing a Strategic Framework,* gave guidance on how joint working could be achieved. Local housing authorities' housing advice services and local arrangements for accessing housing need to be integrated with wider person-centred planning processes for people with learning disabilities. Good liaison is required between landlords and those providing care and support services, where different organisations or staff are involved.

The White Paper, *Valuing People* states that in some areas there has been a lack of active planning by local authorities to develop housing options for people with learning disabilities. In other areas there has been conservatism in the choice of options, with authorities expanding provision by replicating the same type of development rather than taking the opportunity to broaden the range of housing options.

To ensure that this happens, it will be a requirement that new Partnership Boards must produce a local housing strategy, with projections of the number of people with learning disabilities who will need housing in the future. This strategy should also identify the evolving pattern of housing preferences amongst people with learning disabilities locally, and set out plans for the future supply of different housing options, linked in with plans for the future development of care and support services. Guidance on housing and support options will be jointly published by the DTLR and the Office of the Deputy Prime Minister.

Supporting People is a new policy and funding framework for support services that will be implemented in April 2003. It will bring together resources from several existing programmes into a new grant to local authorities, which can be applied more flexibly to fund support services for people with learning disabilities and for other vulnerable people wherever they live. Local social services and housing authorities, working with other partners including the NHS, will be expected to establish joint arrangements for deciding how to apply the new grant and to integrate the planning and commissioning of support services with the planning and commissioning of housing, care, and health services.

Joint strategic planning of supported housing services by local statutory authorities is required for *Supporting People*.[2] Plans will be produced every five years, and the *Supporting People* Strategic Plan must map needs and supply, and link into other strategic plans such as joint investment plans. Housing and social services will jointly form a Core Strategy Development Group which will produce the strategy.

The Housing Corporation will continue to make both revenue and capital allocations for new or remodelled schemes up to 2003. Capital monies from both the Corporation and local authorities will continue to be available for supported housing after 2003, but only where matching revenue resources have been identified from the *Supporting People* revenue pot or elsewhere. Capital investment priorities will be harmonised with the priorities identified in the strategic plan.

[2] Department of Environment, Transport and the Regions, *Supporting People: Policy into Practice* (2001).

9. Glossary

Assistive technology can be simple or sophisticated and includes equipment to aid communication (picture or touch screens), systems for monitoring and control of the person or environment (e.g. alarms, thermostats) or supporting activity (automatic doors, lifts, hoists).

Autistic spectrum disorders describes a range of disability (autism, Kanner's and Asperger's Syndromes) showing common factors of understanding, communication and social behaviour.

Care management A system for organising the management and delivery of care services to vulnerable adults by local authority social services departments, and by CPNs, psychiatrists and other NHS personnel under Care Programme Approach (CPA) for people with mental health problems, involving assessing needs, care planning, organisation of care packages, monitoring and review, and close involvement with users and carers.

Care plan A written statement, regularly updated, setting out the health and social care services that a service user receives through care management, and how it is organised and delivered.

Communal facilities Ancillary communal accommodation, the range of which comprises: common rooms to accommodate tenants and occasional visitors, chair storage and kitchenette for tea-making, warden's office, call systems, laundry and guest rooms.

Direct payments Cash payments to the service user from social services for the purchase of services to meet assessed needs.

Dwelling-house for planning purposes is one occupied by a single person or by people living together as a family, or by not more than six residents living together as a single household (including a household where care is provided for residents).

House in multiple occupation is defined in the Housing Act 1985 (section 345) as a house 'occupied by persons who do not form a single household' and is subject to special fire, management and other standards regulated by the housing department. Interpretation should take into account the size of the group, their relationship to each other and permanence, the extent of sharing and communal living.

Housing Corporation distributes central government housing capital and revenue resources to registered social landlords, regulates their housing activities including ensuring their continued viability, and seeks to promote innovation and good practice.

Housing for the elderly Category 1: self-contained accommodation with an element of warden support and additional communal facilities; Category 2: self-contained accommodation for less active elderly with a warden or 24-hour peripatetic support and additional communal facilities. Frail elderly and extra care supported accommodation, may be either shared or self-contained. This includes warden or 24-hour emergency care, the full range of communal facilities, plus additional special features, including wheelchair user environments and supportive management.

Housing for wheelchair users Accommodation, which may be either shared or self-contained, designed for independent living by physically disabled people and wheelchair users. Where such accommodation is incorporated within schemes containing communal facilities, an appropriate proportion of all such facilities should be wheelchair accessible.

Implementation Support Team has been recruited by the Department of Health with a Director and eight workers, one based in each of the social care regions, to promote effective delivery of *Valuing People*.

Independent advocate An individual who is independent of the home or of any of the statutory agencies involved in the purchasing and provision of care in, or regulation of, the care home, who acts on behalf of and in the interests of a service user who feels unable to represent him/herself when dealing with professionals. Self-advocates are trained and supported to represent their own views.

Joint Investment Plans Plans produced jointly by local authorities, health authorities and other local stakeholders for the integrated provision of services for a range of client groups.

Keyworker The person (who may be a designated nurse for people receiving nursing care) responsible for co-ordinating the service user's plan, for monitoring its progress and for staying in regular contact with the service user and everyone involved.

Learning disability includes the presence of significantly reduced ability to understand new or complex information and to learn new skills, with a reduced ability to cope independently, which started before adulthood with lasting effect on development.

Learning Disability Awards Framework (LDAF) was launched in May 2001 and the aim is that by April 2002 all new entrants to learning disability care services should be registered for qualification with LDAF and by 2005, 50 per cent of front line staff should have achieved at least NVQ level 2.

Learning Disability Development Fund of £22 million revenue and £20 million capital was introduced in April 2002 to support priorities for service change suggested by the White Paper, *Valuing People*. Plans for using the revenue funding and bids for the capital funding should be submitted in joint investment plans.

Learning Disability Partnership Boards have been set up by local councils with social services and should include social services, health bodies (health authorities, NHS Trusts, Primary Care Trusts and/or their successor bodies), housing, education, and the employment service. The Board jointly ensures the appointment of a lead officer to take responsibility for implementing the White Paper, *Valuing People* and for producing a housing strategy.

Lifetime Homes are built to a standard suited to someone with mobility problems but are also more easily and cheaply adapted as needs change. The name derives from the idea that the design features make the house easier to use at each stage in life from childhood to old age.

Out of borough or out of area placements refer to cases where people are placed by the local authority outside their own area either because they need a special service not available locally, because of local shortages of accommodation, or for reasons of cost. Problems can arise subsequently over which local authority takes financial responsibility if people want to move again.

Person-centred planning is a way of helping people work out what they want and how to get it. It looks at what support people will need from those around them, and how this support will be given. It is not just about services but the whole range of support each person requires, from friends, relatives and their community and helping each person to take charge of their own life.

Registered care home An establishment providing accommodation together with personal care, i.e. assistance with bodily functions such as feeding, bathing, and toileting or nursing care.

Reprovision or resettlement Developing alternatives for services or service users formerly in long-stay hospitals, or large residential care homes.

Scheme development standards published by the Housing Corporation provide design guidance for registered social landlords predominantly on affordable general needs housing but including important requirements relating to accessibility, Lifetime Homes, sheltered, shared and supported housing.

Shared housing Accommodation predominantly for single persons, which includes a degree of sharing between tenants of some facilities (e.g. kitchens, bathrooms, living room) and may include an element of support and/or additional communal facilities.

Shared ownership is a housing association programme aimed at people who cannot afford to buy outright but share the ownership with a housing association. The accommodation is partly owned by the occupier and partly rented. The part owned can be purchased with a mortgage (and for disabled people is eligible for income support) and the part owned by the housing association is rented and housing benefit may help pay the rent.

Smart Homes use technology to make it easier for people with physical or sensory limitations to live a normal life in ordinary housing. Controls linked together to form an integrated system can be operated in a variety of ways including manually, by remote infra-red controls, a touch-screen, over the telephone or programmed to operate automatically.

Supported housing Accommodation, which may be either shared or self-contained, designed to meet the special needs of particular user groups (see the Housing Corporation's Guide to Supported Housing) and which includes supportive management and may also include additional communal facilities.

Supporting People is a new policy and funding framework for housing support services that will be implemented in April 2003 bringing together resources from several existing programmes into a new grant to local authorities to fund support services for vulnerable people wherever they live. It does not apply to registered care homes.

Index